# An Introduction to
# Philippine History

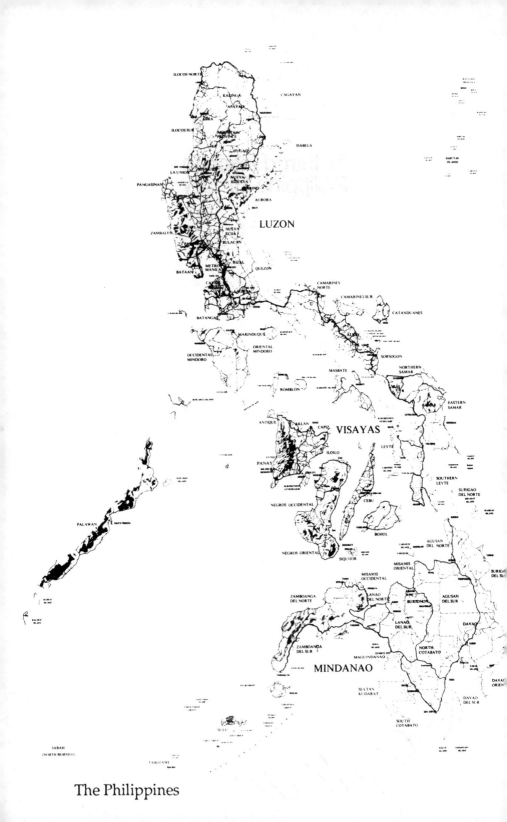

The Philippines

# An Introduction to Philippine History

## JOSÉ S. ARCILLA, S.J.

**FOURTH EDITION ENLARGED**

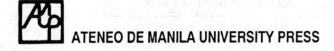

ATENEO DE MANILA UNIVERSITY PRESS

ATENEO DE MANILA UNIVERSITY PRESS
Bellarmine Hall, Katipunan Avenue
Loyola Heights, Quezon City
P.O. Box 154, 1099 Manila, Philippines
Tel.: 426-59-84 / FAX: (632) 426-59-09
E-mail: unipress@pusit.admu.edu.ph

---

The National Library of the Philippines CIP Data

Recommended entry:

Arcilla, Jose S.
    An Introduction to Philippine
history / Jose S. Arcilla. –
4ᵗʰ ed., enl. – Quezon City :
ADMU Press, c1998
    1 v

    1. Philippines – History. I. Title.

DS686.5  959.9  1998
    ISBN 971-550-261-X (pbk.)

# CONTENTS

# PREFACE TO THE FOURTH EDITION

Continuing research and improved teaching methods have refined our understanding of Philippine history. This is why a book first published twenty years ago needs revision. Although essentially the same as its earlier versions, the present text has been updated and enlarged with a few brief excerpts from primary sources of Philippine history.

The need for a more accurate history is felt even outside of the classroom. When society goes through a critical phase, one instinctively asks how things happened and why. One of the best ways to provide a satisfactory answer is to look into history, which explains the roots of any social situation.

A challenge to the classroom teacher is the proper formulation of questions for the students to answer. Instead of offering the class unchallenged statements, the teacher should help students dig up the answers and form the conclusions by themselves. This means the teacher should know enough to be able to guide the students to the sources of knowledge.

One easy way, using the present summary as a starting point, is to introduce students to the primary sources of Philippine history. In this connection, it is wrong to eschew the sources of Philippine history that are authored by Spaniards or Americans and, therefore, allegedly prejudiced in their own favor. Precisely, the test is whether, in spite of blatantly prejudiced and narrow views, the historian can recreate the past as accurately as the sources allow. Without sources, one will never write history, only fiction.

Still convinced of what I noted in the preface of an earlier edition, namely, that teaching is an art, let me add that teaching is really an effort to inspire and help others to strive toward higher ideals. Hence, classroom work is essentially helping the students to rise above themselves, and to read, think, and draw conclusions for themselves.

This does not preclude the use of memory—to many students the bugbear of history classes. The memory is necessary to store basic facts; but more than mere accumulation of facts, the student should be guided to identify the intelligible patterns of history, trace how one element leads to another, or see how one thing resulted from another.

vii

This is history, when one seeks to understand *change and movement in time*. History is indeed a social science; it studies human society. But it should not be identified with sociology. The latter uses a different methodology and analyzes facts from a different viewpoint. Unfortunately, a muddled understanding of these two disciplines has caused much confusion in today's schools, the result of which has not been too healthy for the young.

One hopes this book will help clarify a few forgotten but important concepts.

JOSÉ S. ARCILLA, S.J.

Ateneo de Manila University
Feast of the Divine Motherhood of the Blessed Virgin Mary
1 January 1994

# LIST OF ABBREVIATIONS

BR     Blair, Emma H., and James A. Robertson, *The Philippine Islands, 1493–1898*. 55 vols. Cleveland: Arthur H. Clark.
PS     *Philippine Studies*
PHR   *Pacific Historical Review*

# INTRODUCTION

When applying for a job, you will be asked: "What is your past experience?" Or, "What studies have you completed?"

It is not enough, however, to give an immediate answer. You must prove you are truthful. This means you have to present the evidence, the transcript of academic records and other documents from your alma mater or your former employer.

This question about your past is important. Your future employer will be interested in your background or your personal history in order to understand you.

In a similar way, history, which is research into the past, makes us understand the present. Persons who do not know their country's history will not understand the society they live in. According to Rizal, one who ignores his country's history is someone without a soul.

History is studying the past. Historians' first task is to look for things that survived from the past wherever they can be found. They then go on to ascertain whether these remnants or relics are really genuine artifacts and not fake. Thirdly, historians try to interpret what these survivors of the past mean. Finally, they try to relate them to one another, such that an idea or mental picture is made of the past.

Ideal students of history, therefore, spend their time learning how to search into the past. In this process, the first tool or guide is the class manual. The manual gives the important dates, events, places, and persons that form the skeleton of history. Because history is seldom an accidental chain of unconnected factors, students' main task is to see how one event is related to another. Until this relation has been *traced and understood*, students cannot be said to know the history they are investigating. Any book, for example will tell us that Legazpi conquered Manila in 1571. This is not yet history: this is merely *one fact* of history. Students have to trace, factor by factor, the series of circumstances that ends with the victory of a foreign adventurer over the Muslim confederacy in Manila. History, in other words, is the story of how things happened in the past.

Students, therefore, have a double task: that of identifying and relating basic historical factors. For this task they need the guidance of teachers who, above all, must point out the sources or references of history. They must lead students toward that particular combination of incidents and reasons that starts the events of history.

This book is meant to be an introduction to Philippine history. Emphasis has been to correct the error that history is a calendar to be memorized. With today's flood of printed materials, reference books and outlines are easily obtainable to provide the beginner with the dates, events, persons, and places which are needed in the study of history. It is more important, however, for the student to learn how to analyze the facts and through analysis, understand the past.

The task of students is to READ AND THINK. They must look for the intelligible pattern that brings together the various facts of the past into something that makes sense. Their initial tool is the class manual, which should be the start, not the end, of the discussion. Parallel reading materials should be at hand. History, after all, is a mental discipline that aims to understand how people lived in the past. It is an exercise in judgment, so that in the end we can say, "So, this is what happened."

History is also the story of human emotions. Historical events would never have taken place had people not dreamed, loved, hated, fought for their ideals, and sought to avenge their setbacks or failures. There are historical figures who were greedy and selfish, but there are also those who were generous, courageous, and big-hearted. The true historian will, therefore, understand that the true agents of history are men and women with feelings. Like us, they too wanted the good things to happen and tried to avoid the bad. Their story is our story.

Until recently, history has concentrated on individuals, and the general population has been overlooked. Ordinary people left no written documents or said much that affected their neighbor's life. But these ordinary people who crowded the streets or the battlefields or ships or assembly halls were important. Kingdoms were considered powerful or weak because of the number of their unnamed inhabitants. These people were the ones who fought the king's battles. In times of crisis, they were the ones who endured famine and died from plagues. More importantly perhaps, they were the customers without whom commerce would not have been possible.

In other words, history is the story not just of the individuals we have come to know as leaders or heroes, but especially of the ordinary men, women, and children of each generation. And the Philippines, like all nations, has developed only to the extent that its men, women, and children have acted as one people.

# 1

## IN SEARCH OF SPICES

### The Arrival of the Europeans

On 16 March 1521, a fleet of three ships commanded by Ferdinand Magellan raised eastern Samar. Turning south, the boats dropped anchors off Limasawa Island at the southern tip of Leyte. Two tents for the sick were pitched on the shore. It was Saturday, the feast of Saint Lazarus, and Magellan named the island San Lázaro in his honor.

Two days later, a Monday, nine men beached their boat and walked up to Magellan's makeshift hospital on the shore. Five of them were better dressed than the rest. Magellan forbade his men from moving as he awaited the strangers. Were they friends or enemies?

To the relief of Magellan and his men, the visitors gave "signs of joy because of our arrival," according to the chronicler of the expedition. Some sailed away to call for other companions who were fishing. "On seeing they were reasonable men," Magellan offered them food and drink.

This was the first meeting between the islanders of the future Philippines and the Europeans who traveled west in order to reach the spice islands (today eastern Indonesia) in the east. About thirty years earlier, on 12 October 1492, Christopher Columbus had reached the island (today Haiti and the Dominican Republic) which he named San Salvador—and which he thought was China.

To his dying day, the discoverer insisted he was right. But in 1513, Vasco Nuñez de Balboa proved him wrong. After hiking across the isthmus of Panama, Balboa saw, as he looked southward from Mount Darien, a huge body of water which he called "Southern Sea" and claimed for the Castilian crown.

Surprised and overjoyed at the same time, Balboa proved that Columbus had not found China, but an unknown continent blocking a direct route to the east. In order, therefore, to reach the eastern spiceries, one had to find a passage through this huge land mass. Seven years later, in 1520, Magellan discovered this passage (today called the Strait of Magellan in his honor) and a few months later, on 16 March 1521, reached the future Philippines.

1

In Limasawa, the islanders and the Europeans quickly became friends. The islanders described to the newcomers other places, like Butuan and Calagan (Caraga), but Magellan did not go there. Cebu was also mentioned, and a week later, the Europeans, guided northwestward by the Limasawa chief, sailed past Leyte, Bohol, Camiguin, Baybay on western Leyte, and Gatighan, a place hard to identify today.

On 7 April 1521, a Sunday, the European fleet entered the narrow sea between Mactan and Cebu. Magellan ranged his ships in battle formation and fired all his guns, scaring the Cebuanos. Actually, Magellan was just following the European custom of saluting the people on arrival at friendly ports. He was honoring the local chief.

On landing, Magellan's interpreter explained they had come to "discover Malucho; but that he had come solely to visit the king [of Cebu] because of the good report which he had heard of him from the king of Mazawa, and to buy food with his merchandise." This was probably diplomatic doubletalk, but the Cebuano spokesman replied they were welcome. But Chief Saripada Humabon demanded they must first pay the tribute or *buwis* imposed on all incoming ships. Magellan refused, boasting he represented a great king who paid no tributes. They might regret it, Magellan threatened, if they insisted on collecting payment.

A Moro trader warned the Cebuano leader the newcomers were subjects of a powerful king who had already conquered Calicut, Malaca, and all of India. He was referring, of course, to the Portuguese king and not to King Charles V (1516–1556) of Spain. But the trader knew no better, and Magellan did not disabuse him. The chief bade the Europeans to wait till he could consult his advisers the next morning, but in the meantime offered them "refreshments of many dishes, all made from meat and contained in porcelain platters, besides many jars of wine."

The next day, Monday, at a formal meeting between the Cebuanos and the visitors, Magellan's interpreter assured the former that the Europeans "wished only to trade." Satisfied, the Cebuano leader offered his friendship. As a token, he asked Magellan to "send him a drop of blood from his right arm, and he himself would do the same, as the sign of the most sincere friendship."

Magellan, therefore, came in peace, seeking trade and not conquest. During his brief stay in Cebu, he mentioned many things that sounded new to the Cebuano chief, adding that he prayed to "God to confirm . . . in heaven" their new friendship. For Humabon, this was a novel, but pleasant experience.

Asked who would succeed the chief when he died, Humabon explained he had no son, only daughters. The eldest was married to his nephew. This man was the *rajamuda* or crown prince expected to succeed to the throne. Magellan was also told that "when the fathers and mothers grow old, they received no further honor, but their children commanded them."

Magellan grabbed the chance to explain the Christian law of love and respect for parents and elders, even if they were old and weak. He also narrated the Bible story of creation, of Adam and Eve, of life after death, and other Christian beliefs. Because he could not leave behind teachers to instruct the Cebuanos, Magellan offered to baptize them, if they wanted, and to bring priests the next time to teach them the Christian religion in greater depth.

The Cebuanos did not wait for Magellan's return before they embraced Christianity. On 14 April, a week after the arrival of Europeans, Humabon was baptized in a plaza on a platform blessed and adorned with banners and palm branches. Magellan gave him the name Don Carlos, in honor of the Spanish king, and assured him "he would more easily conquer his enemies than before." No explanation was given as to how Humabon would become more powerful as a subject of Spain.

## Magellan's Death

When Humabon (now Don Carlos) reported that "some of the chiefs did not wish to obey him, because they said they were as good men as he," Magellan had "all the chiefs of the king called, and told them that, unless they obeyed" Humabon as their king, Magellan "would have them killed and would give their possessions to the king."

About 400 Cebuanos were soon baptized, among them Humabon's wife, who received the Christian name of Doña Juana, in honor of the Castilian queen. She had earlier seen an image of Our Lady, a beautiful wooden statue of the Child Jesus (Santo Niño), and a crucifix, and was "overcome with contrition and asked for the baptism amid her tears." Historians believe that the Santo Niño image venerated in Cebu today is Magellan's gift to the sultana of Cebu, or Doña Juana, to call her by her Christian name.

On 26 April, Zula, one of the chiefs of Mactan, an island off Cebu, sent Magellan a gift of two goats, apologizing that he could not offer more since Lapulapu, another Mactan chief, had refused to "obey the king of Spain." But Zula assured Magellan that with European reenforcements he could subdue his rival. Rather than dispatch reenforcements, Magellan, against prudent advice, volunteered to fight Lapulapu. Magellan did not foresee it, but his desire to help a submissive chief would lead to his own death.

About three o'clock the next morning, Magellan, with sixty fighters, reached Mactan. But he neither took the normal battle precaution to reconnoiter unknown terrain, nor provided for adequate fire support in an amphibious military operation on the Mactan shore. Moreover, he did not immediately strike as soon as he arrived, waiting instead for the sun to rise before striking. He even allowed the enemy to summon allies, thus outnumbering the Europeans.

Under the bright morning sun, the fight did not last long. The native arrows which came down like rain were more effective than the Spanish cannonballs which did not destroy, but merely flew through, the flimsy nipa walls of the Mactan huts. Because their guns were inflicting no damage, Magellan ordered some of his men to burn the huts. This further enraged the islanders. The Europeans panicked as more and more Mactan warriors encircled them in the shallow sea. Magellan commanded an orderly retreat, but his voice was drowned out by the noise of the waves and the shouting. He was soon recognized as the leader, and the warriors surrounded him. Pigafetta described Magellan's final hour:

> Recognizing the captain, so many turned upon him that they knocked his helmet off his head twice, but he always stood firmly like a good knight, with some others. Thus did we fight for more than one hour. An Indian hurled a bamboo spear into the captain's face, but the latter immediately killed him with his lance, which he left in the Indian's body. Then, trying to lay hand on sword, he could draw it out but halfway, because he had been wounded in the arm with a bamboo spear. When the natives saw that, they all hurled themselves upon him. One of them wounded him on the left leg with a large cutlass. . . . That caused the captain to fall downward, when they immediately rushed upon him with iron and bamboo spears and with their cutlasses, until they killed our mirror, our light, our comfort, and our true guide. When they wounded him, he turned back many times to see whether we were all in the boats. Thereupon, beholding him dead, we, wounded, retreated, as best as we could, to the boats which were already pulling off.

One wonders why so much has been made of the "heroic valor" of Lapulapu, for paradoxically, it was Magellan's own courage and self-confidence which destroyed him. Several military blunders explain not the heroism of the Mactan fighters but Magellan's defeat. His friends failed to dissuade him from fighting in terrain he had not previously reconnoitered, omitting a basic military tactic. He had allowed the enemy to outnumber his small band of about sixty soldiers. He had not attacked the moment he reached Mactan. Moreover, no document mentions that it was Lapulapu who plunged the weapon that snuffed out Magellan's life. And even if it had been he, by his leadership, who had killed the Portuguese navigator, Lapulapu did not do so in defense of the Philippines, for that nation as yet *did not exist.*

## Voyages after Magellan

Magellan died on 27 April 1521, and Juan Sebastián del Cano (some say Elcano), a subordinate officer who had mutinied against him, steered the remaining boat, the *Victoria*, back to Spain. On 6 September 1522, with only eighteen of the sixty survivors who had escaped to the Moluccas from Cebu, she docked at Sevilla. The next day, the haggard expeditionaries went on pilgrimage, barefoot, each with a lighted candle, to the shrines of Our Lady of Victory and Saint Mary of Antiquity in thanksgiving for their return. In circumnavigating the world for the first time, they had survived the horrors of 14,460 leagues (or about 52,300 kilometers) of unknown bodies of water.

Their arrival proved there was indeed a western route to the far eastern spiceries. The spice they had brought home more than paid for the original expenses of the expedition.

Three years later, in 1525, Jofre García de Loaysa headed a fleet of seven sail. His orders were to take the same route opened by Magellan. But disaster struck immediately. A heavy storm destroyed one boat and blew away two. Only four remained when Loaysa guided his fleet through Magellan's strait. Barely out on the Pacific, another storm hit them. The *Victoria*, the same boat that had circumnavigated the world, was separated from the other three, two of which were never heard from again.

As though the storms were not enough, the scurvy plagued the crew and many died from the disease. On 30 July 1526, Loaysa died. Sebastián del Cano took command, but in four days, he also died. Alonso de Salazar was next in line. He succeeded in guiding the decimated expedition to a bay in Mindanao which the Spaniards called *Vizcaya*, probably what is now Lianga Bay off Surigao.

To ascertain the fate of Loaysa and his expedition, a fleet was readied in Mexico under the command of Álvaro Saavedra de Cerón. Departing on 31 October 1527, the fleet sighted the islets off Surigao on 1 February 1528. But the hostile inhabitants forced the Spaniards to sail on. Along the way, the fleet picked up some stragglers from the ill-fated Loaysa expedition. At Tidore, one of the spice islands (today part of Indonesia), the Spaniards stopped for spices and turned eastward for the trip back to Mexico.

That was their mistake. On that lower latitude, contrary winds blew them back, and try as they might, they failed to go farther. When they finally hit the Caroline Islands, Saavedra died and Pedro Laso took command of the ship. A week later, he too died. The third captain gave up and surrendered to the Portuguese in Tidore.

Shortly after, another Spanish expedition was entrusted to Ruy López de Villalobos. It sought the Philippine Islands, not the Moluccas, for by this time, the claims of Portugal and Spain had been settled by the Treaty of Zaragoza. On 1 November 1542, Villalobos left Mexico and arrived at Baganga Bay in Davao Oriental on 2 February 1543. They set out again to look for food in Limasawa, but strong winds drove them back. They reached Sarangani Bay in southern Mindanao, but they found little to eat. They finally decided to proceed to Tidore and, on 24 April 1544, like the rest, surrendered to the Portuguese. Villalobos died the next day.

All their expeditions had failed, but the Spaniards learned something important: There was indeed a western route to the eastern spiceries, but it was too long, and supplies could not last the trip. But if there were stations where the ships could anchor and revictual, the western route might be feasible. But how would they return? This was the next question.

## Suggestions for Further Reading

*(Complete information on recommended readings appears in the bibliography at the end of the book.)*

Morison, Samuel E., *Admiral of the ocean sea: A life of Christopher Columbus*; Pigafetta, Antonio, "Magellan's voyage around the world," in *BR 33–34*.

# 2

## THE CONQUEST OF THE PHILIPPINES

### The Legazpi Expedition

In 1559, at the suggestion of the viceroy in Mexico, King Philip II of Spain ordered the equipment of a new expedition to the Philippines, as the islands of Samar and Leyte were called in his honor by Villalobos. The name soon applied to the entire archipelago. Newly crowned, Philip wanted to strengthen the Spanish claim to the eastern spiceries.

Meanwhile, Urdaneta, now an Augustinian priest, was saying—because of his earlier experience as Loaysa's page—that it was easy to sail west to reach the east and return by the same route. And because of his experience and confidence, he was asked to join the expedition as chief pilot. At Urdaneta's suggestion, Miguel López de Legazpi, a royal official in Mexico with an unblemished record, was named its commander.

Legazpi's instructions were, in part,

> to bring to the inhabitants of those places our Holy Catholic Faith and to discover the return route to New Spain to the credit and patrimony of the Royal Crown of Castile, through trade and barter and through other legitimate ways, which with a clear conscience should be carried on to bring back some spices and some of the wealth found in those places.

Preparations began on 24 September 1559 and, after some delay, the fleet set sail on 20 November 1564. There were four ships: *San Pedro* (the flagship or *capitana*), *San Pablo*, *San Juan de Letrán*, and *San Lucas*. No native Americans were allowed on board; no women. Five Augustinian missionaries accompanied the expedition: Frs. Andrés de Urdaneta, Diego de Herrera, Martín de Rada, Andrés de Aguirre, and Pedro de Gamboa. Two hours after midnight, the expedition lifted anchors, unfurled sails, and set out on a western route to the east.

The Pacific Ocean was exactly that: pacific, easy to sail. On 8 January 1565, land was sighted and a cannonball was fired, but it proved to be a mirage. Next day, actual land was sighted, now known as the Barbados

Islands because its people were bearded. Guam was reached two weeks later. Legazpi took possession in the king's name, and the expeditionaries bartered for a few things. On 3 February, they sailed again and, ten days later, they saw rising from the sea the eastern coast of Samar.

Contrary to what they had expected, the people were unfriendly. In Cabalian, in Limasawa, in Camiguin, and in Butuan, the natives fled as soon as the Spaniards arrived. Further on, they captured a Borneo vessel, but Legazpi ordered its cargo returned to the owners. Then its Moro pilot explained to them the reason for the natives' hostility: the Portuguese had poisoned the minds of the eastern Visayans. Friendly at first, and introducing themselves as Spaniards, the Portuguese were welcomed by the natives. But soon, they turned against the population, burning fields and effectively turning the natives against the Spaniards.

The lack of food had become a serious problem. Several scouting groups had gone out, and two men, Esteban Rodríguez de Figueroa and Juan de Aguirre, returned with glowing reports about a big port called Sugbu. On 25 August 1565, the Spanish fleet entered this big port. But because the Sugbuanons refused to receive them peacefully, Legazpi used their cannons and bombarded the town, causing the natives to scamper to the hills, leaving their houses in flames. When the Spaniards landed unopposed, they found an image of the Child Jesus. Some believe it was Magellan's gift to the sultana of Cebu when she was baptized forty-four years before.

Legazpi lost no time in starting a Spanish town, assigning lots to the Augustinians and building a triangular encampment on what is probably today San Nicolas district in Cebu.

One day, a soldier ventured out alone, and the Cebuanos immediately speared him to death. In retaliation, a posse set out and captured about forty prisoners, among them the niece of Chief Tupas of Cebu.

When told who she was, Legazpi sent her yaya to tell the chief to come and take back the prisoners, but that he should make peace with the Spaniards.

Tupas did not appear; the girl's father did. He came with six of his own retinue to offer themselves as slaves since his daughter, he thought, had already been enslaved. Among the islanders, this was the usual treatment given to prisoners captured in war.

Legazpi assured the man he did not have to worry, and had the girl brought out, clothed as befitting her royal rank, a princess, to her father's utter amazement.

This won him over. No, he told Legazpi, he was not going to take back his daughter. Instead, he was going back to tell his brother, Tupas, to befriend the Spaniards. Otherwise, he would kill the chief, as he had men to do it for him.

This incident is hardly mentioned by historians, but it was important. It was a totally novel experience for Tupas's brother, who had expected the worst for his daughter. But Legazpi honored her as a noble lady. He also treated the other prisoners humanely even if they were his captives taken in combat.

This action taught the girl's father a different meaning of life. Till then, to settle difficulties, he usually employed the *kampilan*, the spear, or the bow and arrow. He had not yet known of the Christian view of the human person. Life was cheap, and he did not hesitate to kill in order to carry out his wishes.

For the first time, through actions and not merely words, the Cebuanos witnessed a nobler way of acting. As the missionaries would later explain to them, Christianity offered a better life. Trading was one purpose of Legazpi's expedition, but the Cebuanos too were introduced to new ways of thinking and behaving.

Tupas finally made peace with the Spaniards. He promised to be a loyal and faithful "vassal" of the Spanish crown, and to obey the royal commands and orders from its representative, the governor general of the Philippines. He also agreed to help fight the king's enemies. The Spaniards in turn assured him they would do the same. As a sign of their vassalage, the Cebuanos would pay a tribute, or *pagdatu*, long practiced among the islanders.

Peaceful alliance, however, did not solve the problem of shortage of food. Martín de Goyti and Mateo de Saz, Legazpi's trusted officers, made trips to Negros and Leyte Islands, but they obtained little to satisfy their needs. In 1570, they went northwards to Manila and conquered it after a brief skirmish.

In the meantime, Legazpi transferred his headquarters to Panay, hoping to find more food there. It also seemed a better place to defend themselves against the Portuguese who had twice threatened them.

And from there, following royal instructions, Legazpi sent a boat back to Mexico, piloted by Fray Andrés de Urdaneta. Instead of going directly east on the lower latitudes, he first steered northward to Japan. There he turned east, sailing before the northwest wind till the western coast of America. Turning south off the California coast, he reached Acapulco after only five months and eight days at sea, sooner than the eight month he had thought the return trip would take. Urdaneta had successfully made the return trip to Mexico. For the next three centuries, this was the route that tied the Philippines to the Spanish royal government:

westward to the Philippines on the lower latitudes, eastward to Mexico on the higher.

Urdaneta's boat arrived in Acapulco on 8 October 1565, an important date in Philippine history. Now, the farthest colony of Spain could be linked to the home government. This convinced King Philip to order Legazpi to stay in the archipelago and begin *pacifying* the Filipinos to convert them to the Catholic faith.

Painful experience in South America had taught the Spaniards they were not justified in *conquering* other peoples, especially if through bloody means. But if the crown helped spread the Gospel of Christ, the Spaniards could in conscience colonize and impose their own government on the Filipinos. That is why the royal instructions mentioned "pacification," and hardly "conquest." We shall learn more about of this later.

In 1571, Legazpi decided to sail to Manila. Everyone had been speaking highly about that port; and if the Spaniards intended to proceed with their plan to conquer China, it would serve as a strategic stepping stone.

They were in Manila about 15 May, but the *adelantado* (advance officer) was in no haste to land. He worried that because of the treatment the Manileños received from Goyti the year before, they might be unfriendly. For four days, he negotiated and held talks with two friendly chiefs of Manila, the *matanda* (elder), and Lakandula. Both became convinced the Spaniards were coming in peace, and the two agreed to live in peace with them. Only Raja Soliman held out, probably because of what had happened the previous year. But when he was assured there would be no reprisals, he declared, although probably with reservations, that he too was willing to receive the Spaniards in peace.

Assured of a peaceful reception, Legazpi landed and took possession of Manila. He performed the symbolic ceremony of lopping off tree branches as a sign of ownership. It was 18 May 1571. He had conquered, not by force of arms, but by diplomacy and tact, and by respecting the rights of the natives.

It was not as easy as it looked. The chiefs regretted losing their power and challenged the Spaniards in many ways. They boasted they, too, had their own gods. However, if the Christian God proved Himself stronger, they were willing to accept Spanish rule. Though native defenses were not to be despised, Spanish artillery and military tactics eventually wore down native resistance. And convinced the Christian God was more powerful than theirs, the settlements around Laguna de Bay submitted to the new rulers.

## Prehispanic Islands

Today, the Republic of the Philippines is one nation, but it is perhaps the most divided geographically. It is an archipelago of about 7,100 islands located 966 kilometers south of China, between 4 and 21 degrees north latitude, and 116 and 127 degrees east longitude. Its northernmost island is only 240 kilometers south of Taiwan, its southernmost, 24 north of Borneo.

From north to south, the Philippines is 1,851 kilometers long, and 1,107 kilometers from east to west. If connected end to end, all the islands placed together would measure 300,000 square kilometers.

The country is divided into three groups: Luzon, the biggest, in the north, measuring 141,395 square kilometers; Visayas, the smallest, in the middle, with 56,606 square kilometers; and Mindanao, the second largest, in the south, totaling 101,100 square kilometers.

There are 4,327 islands with no names, but not all the 2,773 islands that do have them are fully inhabited. Some of the smallest islands are mere rocks or huge coral appearing above the sea, with perhaps a few coconut or other palm trees.

The Philippines is at the base of a fan opening out to the southeast Asian semicircle on the western edge of the Pacific Ocean. Strategically located, our country serves as a buffer for lands farther west. The Philippines on the lower latitude is the first huge land mass reached by sailors from the eastern Pacific, the first hit by typhoons blowing in from the ocean, and the last significant landfall when sailing eastward. Policymakers have not missed this detail.

The Philippines is made up of high mountain ranges that divide the country into roughly a western and an eastern half. The lowlands are narrow coastal strips or valleys between the mountains, the biggest of which are the Central Plain and Cagayan Valley in Luzon, and Agusan Valley and Cotabato Valley in Mindanao.

The country's climate alternates between a rainy and a dry season. Briefly, from November to April, western Luzon, Mindoro, Negros, and Palawan have a dry season. The rest of the year is rainy. The eastern sector of the archipelago has a wet or rainy season from November to April, but a dry one during the rest of the year.

The development of the Philippines has been affected by its climate. For example, heavy humidity and rainfall most of the year help spread certain diseases. Typhoons have always disturbed the economic programs of the government. And located on the earthquake belt, with a large number of volcanoes, the Philippines has seen its plans for modernization often ruined or delayed by the onset of natural disasters.

## Oldest Signs of Human Society

We are told human beings lived in what is now the Philippines as early as 50,000 years ago. This was in the Pleistocene Era, when ice covered a great part of the earth, and the sea level was lower than it is today, revealing wider dry areas. What are today just islands rising from the sea were solid land connected with mainland Asia. People could wander on foot from one place to another, carrying cutting instruments of flaked or sharply broken chert, or pebbles from the rivers. No signs of sea food have been found in the sites inhabited by the earliest Philippine dwellers, and scholars tell us they probably ate only bats, birds, or small mammals.

Between 3,000 and 1,000 years ago, the ice covering much of the earth melted and the sea level rose, leaving extensive regions under water, except the higher areas, now the islands forming the Philippine archipelago. Human beings, however, continued to arrive and leave the Philippines, some sailing to as far as the Pacific Islands today. They were food gatherers, hunters, and fishers. With their thin-edged cutters and stone hammers, they killed birds and bats for food.

In the next geological period whose date one cannot determine exactly, improved tools enabled people to cut down trees and open wider spaces for tilling crops, like rice, taro, and other edible roots. People could move around more freely, generally in primitive sailing craft. They beat tree barks into clothing and made adzes from thick shells.

The oldest pottery found in the country is dated 1500 B.C. The first tools of bronze, copper, and some gold go back to 500 or 400 B.C. Because the Philippines had no tin, there were hardly any bronze instruments, and the next period is characterized by tools made of iron, glass, and nephryte.

By this time, clothing of beaten bark was replaced by abaca woven in looms, perhaps like the ones still found in the Mountain Province or Mindanao. The population increased, some occupying coastal areas protected by outlying islands, like Davao protected by Samal, Cebu by Mactan, and Manila by Corregidor. Other settlements were along the rivers, called *ríos poblados* (inhabited or settled rivers) by the first Spaniards in the country. There were several reasons why people chose habitats close to a body of water: for defense, transportation, or food which was mostly fish, shellfish, and crustaceans. When a Jesuit missionary first arrived in Cebu and Bohol in the 1640s, he still saw the *harigues* or posts of ancient houses sticking up from the sea near the shore.

The earliest traders in the Philippines were the Chinese and the Arabs. However, even before their coming, the natives had been making their own jars for burial ceremonies or fermenting rice wine. But the better dragon-designed brown stone jars brought from China slowly replaced the local jars.

Small and large jars found by the archaeologists show that "primary" and "secondary" burial rites were observed. In the first, the dead was placed in a large jar until the flesh rotted and disintegrated. The bones were then disinterred, cleaned, washed, and even painted, before being reburied in a smaller jar. This was the secondary burial.

This practice of honoring the dead shows that the prehispanic tribes believed in life after death. Religion was taught through verses chanted for sailing, working in the fields, or mourning the dead.

It is from the first Spanish reports that we know about the more specific religious practices before the missionaries came. For example, a priestly class of twelve ranks existed, or religious festivals were observed in the islands. And yet, there were no permanent places for worship, like churches or temples. On the other hand, cemeteries were especially honored and guarded.

The supreme god was (in Tagalog) *Bathala*, a name similar to the Indian *Berhala* or Malayan Sanskrit *Batara* and, therefore, indicating that part of Philippine culture was derived from the Indians or the Malayans.

## Suggestions for Further Reading

*(Complete information on recommended readings appears in the bibliography at the end of the book.)*

Noone, Martin J., *The islands saw it: The discovery and conquest of the Philippines, 1521–1581;* Morga, Antonio de, "Sucesos de las Islas Filipinas," in *BR* 15–16; Scott, William H., *Prehispanic source materials for the study of Philippine history*.

# 3

## THE NEW COLONY

### Gente Sin Policía

Recent studies point to the need to modify the early descriptions of indigenous society by the first Spaniards in the Philippines. First, although similar in many ways, the prehispanic tribes were not a homogeneous group. Each region or tribe in the Visayas or Luzon had its own admirable local culture; there was still no unified Philippine society.

One thing quickly impressed the Europeans, namely, the lack of a supreme authority that ruled all the tribes as a single political entity. Instead, neighboring tribes were constantly fighting one another. For example, as mentioned, Zula of Mactan had no power over Lapulapu, his fellow chief in the same island of Mactan. Humabon told Magellan not all the chiefs in Cebu obeyed him. In 1565, Legazpi reported to the Spanish king that "the people do not act in concert or obey any ruling body; but each man does whatever he pleases, and takes care only of himself and of his slaves."

The same lack of unity also impressed the notary who recorded the first meeting between Martín de Goyti and the chiefs of Manila in 1570:

> Soon after came the other ruler, his nephew Soliman, who was a younger man. . . . Soliman assumed an air of importance and haughtiness and said that he was pleased to be the friend of the Spaniards, but the latter should understand they were not painted Indians. He said that they would not tolerate any abuse, as had the others; on the contrary they would repay with death the least thing that touched their honor.

In other words, Soliman was telling the Spaniards his people were Taga-ilog, or Tagalog, different from the painted, or tattooed, Visayans who had already surrendered to the foreigners. For, isolated in islands, or separated from one another by roadless mountains and rivers, they had little or no contact with one another. Only the few traders had access to places other than their own *bayan*. This partly explains why, until now, there are more than a hundred variations of the major Philippine idioms.

When the Spaniards arrived in the late sixteenth century, the Tagalog social ranking was different from the Visayan. The former had four levels, while the latter only three. Both the Tagalogs and the Visayans had a *datu* class, which by 1650 had come to be called the *principalia*.

The Tagalog datus were the *maginoo* who ruled a *barangay (nagdarato)* or a barrio *(dolohan)*. The Tagalog datu was like a barangay or boat pilot whose commands had to be obeyed lest the boat sink. He ruled between thirty to a hundred families in the bayan, later called *pueblo* by the Spaniards. Only through the male line could one succeed to the datu's throne. The datu's main obligations were to rule his people, lead them in fighting or defending the barangay, and render judgment in disputes. In return, he received honors and part of the harvests of his followers, who also worked for him on special days.

The Visayan datu did not differ much from the Tagalog, and both depended on the loyalty and service of the lower social classes, the *timawa* or *maharlika* among the Tagalogs, and the *timawa* or *tumao* among the Visayans. Like the Tagalog datu, the Visayan chief had special privileges. If captured, his followers were obliged to ransom him. He also collected tribute and ruled over the barrio, variously called *sakop, haop,* or *dolohan*. He was the leader in tribal fights, called *mangubat, managayau* (land fights), or *mangahat* (sea fights).

The Tagalog timawa, called *hidalgos* by the first Spanish writers, had their own rights, like harvesting without paying the tribute, or having followers other than those of the datu's. They were either the illegitimate children of the datus, or members of the lower class who purchased their freedom or paid their debts.

The maharlika were the datu's fighters. But they supplied their own weapons and other fighting equipment. They received a share in the spoils and received services from others in the barangay. By about 1630, when chronic tribal fighting ended, the original maharlika class had disappeared.

The Visayan tumao (which means "be manly") were descendants of former datus who had no taint of slavery, servitude, or witchcraft. From them, the datu appointed the chief officials, the *atubang sa datu* or prime minister, and the *sandig sa datu* or datu's supporters. The Visayan *timawa* referred to the illegitimate children of the datu's concubines, called *binokot*. They had no privileges, but were free. On their father's death they were called *ginoo*. By 1650, the word had come to merely mean "tribute payer," while among the Tagalogs, it had become equivalent to the modern English title, "sir."

The first Spanish reports mentioned a local "middle class" which was actually various levels of free members of the barangay or tribe mentioned above. Below them were the Tagalog *alipin* or Visayan *oripun*, also of several levels. These were not slaves, but members of the lower level of local society.

The Tagalogs recognized the rights of the *alipin namamahay* which included the right to plant their own crops. *Namamahay* means "householder," and this class had rights to some piece of land. However, these rights were revoked if they were found guilty of a crime. And unless condemned to die, they were sentenced to perpetual enslavement. A second group was the *alipin sa gigilid*, or "hearth slaves." These included captives taken in battle, or purchased slaves.

The first group lived in their own houses, while the second in their master's. The alipin sa gigilid could be sold or transferred to another master as payment of a debt. For convenience, the alipin sa gigilid were freed and allowed to live in their own house when they married. They could also buy their freedom if they worked, for example, as a goldsmith and saved the equivalent of 30 pesos to 90 pesos or even more.

The Visayan oripun were the commoners, who could not marry into the datu class. They were usually agricultural workers. Some were rich, but others were even poorer than the slaves. Some of them had no rights at all and were fed only to serve later as human sacrificial victims or be buried alive with the jewels and weapons of a dead master.

Finally, the lowest level of indigenous society were those called, among the Visayans, the *tumataban* or *tumaranpok*. Of these, the most enslaved were the *ayuey* (or *hayohey*), who served in the master's house three out of four days. The *tuhey* were slaves who became free after marriage, while the *lubus nga oripun* were those who handed over their entire harvest to the master.

Because the Spaniards immediately tried to change local society, traditional class groups soon disappeared, and it is now not easy to define exactly the distinctive characteristics of each. But it is clear that prehispanic society was divided into the chiefly and the nonchiefly ranks. The first included the high chiefs (for example, datu) and the low chiefs (timawa or atubang sa datu). The nonchiefs included the slaves who obtained their freedom, those burdened with unpaid debts, and the chattel slaves.

But social distinctions were not watertight. Datus had to prove they were capable of ruling, or else someone better or stronger could displace him.

## Unification into One Colony

The first task of the Spaniards in the country was to unify the people under one religious faith and one government with its seat in Manila. The prehispanic datus and barangays were preserved, but the datu became the "barangay head" (*cabeza de barangay*), whose main duties were to collect the tribute and recruit the men, or *polistas* for corvée or public service.

Each barangay, later called *gremio*, had forty to fifty families, all listed in the *padron* or the *mapa de almas* drawn up by the parish priests. Both lists helped in tribute collection and in checking, at least in the beginning, how faithfully the baptized Filipinos fulfilled their religious obligations, like attending Sunday Mass and going to confession at least once a year.

Several contiguous barangays were united under one local government. They could be one or several *barrios*, a barrio being a group of houses close together and bigger than the *visita*. The latter did not have its own civil officials, but the former did.

At first, people living together in one place were in the charge of an *encomendero*, a Spaniard who, for a commission, received all the local tributes from the barangay heads and assigned certain males to specific public services called the *polo*. When the annual tributes totaled 500 or more, the pueblo was erected as a *municipio*, whose top official was a *gobernadorcillo*, equivalent to today's town mayor. He was assisted by four lower officials: the *teniente mayor* or town deputy, the *juez de policía* charged with peace and order, the *juez de sementeras* in charge of lands and crops, and the *juez de ganados*, in charge of livestock and the butchering of animals for sale.

Several municipios formed an *alcaldía* (later *provincia*) governed by the *alcalde mayor* (later *gobernador provincial*). The latter could not enact laws, but merely implemented orders forwarded through the Manila office from Spain. He hardly made any decisions, although he recommended certain measures to the governor general in Manila.

By 1700, there were twelve alcaldes in the Philippines who each received a yearly salary of only 300 pesos, which not rarely made them look for other sources of income, honestly or dishonestly. For example, court cases involving not more than 200 pesos were appealed to the alcalde from the sala of the gobernadorcillo. But when the presiding judge was the alcalde himself, there was no guarantee the sentence would be just.

By 1885, the alcalde mayor was called *gobernador civil*, to distinguish him from the *gobernador politico-militar* (politicomilitary governor). He exercised various functions: provision of adequate food supply, maintenance of good roads and bridges, issuance of commercial licenses and permits, approval of monopolies (that is, sale of rum, control of cockfighting galleries, etc.), supervision of municipal elections, and promotion of the people's religious welfare.

The politicomilitary governor was assigned to regions that had not yet been fully conquered. Besides his civil functions, he also exercised those of a military commander.

The top royal official in the Philippines was the governor general. He was the royal mouthpiece, acting for the king who was absolute lord of the entire Spanish world, and for the Council of the Indies which assisted the crown in everything regarding the colonies. Like the alcalde mayor, the governor general did not promulgate laws for the Philippines, which was an exclusive royal prerogative.

However, because of the distance, the governor in Manila was practically independent from the king, and could disregard laws which were inapplicable to local conditions. In this situation, he suggested amendments. And until the royal directives reached Manila, these were not followed. Hence, there developed the legal tradition, "a la ley se acata, no se cumple" (we revere the law, but do not carry it out). Given the means of communication at that period, there was always room for abuse. If the governor was good, everything was fine; otherwise, there could be any number of problems.

The term "governor" simply meant one in charge of a *gobernación*. He was also called "president," because he presided over the meetings of the audiencia, or the supreme court and council of judges *(oidores)*. Until 1898, there remained unconquered regions not effectively under Spanish control, and therefore need of an active armed forces. The governor was hence also titled "captain general" and acted as the supreme commander of the armed forces, assisted by the *segundo cabo* or deputy commander.

Finally, the governor general was the "vice-patron" of the church in all of Asia. As such, he nominated new bishops and approved financial assistance for the missions.

Perhaps more importantly, the governor general also controlled the colonial treasury. In 1784, this office was removed from his control. As will be seen later, this would become a probable factor in the Cavite Mutiny of 1872.

The governor general, therefore, had extensive powers: judicial, financial, military, and religious. To avoid abuse, there were three checks on him. The Archbishop of Manila was ideally the moral conscience of the colony. As a matter of fact, Philippine history is filled with stories of the clashes and disagreements between these two top authorities of the colony.

The second check on the governor was the *audiencia*. Inaugurated in 1583 because of the governor's almost absolute control of the colony, it was dissolved six years later for lack of resources to pay the oidores' salaries. But in 1595, it had to be restored, precisely as a check for abusive royal officials.

There were four oidores under the presidency of the governor himself. The audiencia also included a *fiscal* (prosecuting attorney), an *alguacil mayor* (chief constable), and a *teniente de gran canciller* (deputy of the chief chancellor). They met three times a week, but because of low salaries, they were not immune to bribery or personal vindictiveness.

Besides advising the governor, the audiencia reviewed his actuations and, in cases of vacancy, ruled the colony in civil affairs. It was also the supreme colonial court of justice.

The third check on the governor general as well as on the other colonial officials was the special court called *juicio de residencia*. At the end of one's tenure, a special court was convened to review past actuations of the outgoing royal official. A public announcement was made and all were invited to present their testimony in court. If guilty, the officials were penalized with imprisonment, confiscation of property, fines, or all of these together. Unfortunately, the *juez de residencia* was often also the incoming royal appointee. Knowing he himself would stand trial after his term of service, it was not easy for him to issue impartial sentences.

The Spanish colonies were at first divided into two viceroyalties: New Spain and Peru. The Philippines belonged to the first, which is why both royal decrees from Spain and official decisions from the Philippines were mediated by the viceroy in Mexico City.

In the appointment to royal offices, provincial posts could be obtained by paying a fixed sum of money. Spain was almost always bankrupt, and the sale of offices not connected with the administration of justice was a big source of royal income. An office was sold at public auction *(pública almoneda)*; and the one who won the bidding either paid in full or gave a down of only a third of the cost, with the balance to be liquidated later. But until royal confirmation was granted, the office remained vacant.

The most popular office with a salary was that of the *escribano público*, provincial or municipal scribe. Rodrigo de Quadros paid 1,000 pesos for the Pampanga *escribanía*, while Ramírez de Alarcón paid only 800 pesos for the same position in Mindoro. But Captain Martín de Esquivel paid 20,000 pesos for the post of chief constable of the Manila audiencia. People, of course, paid for these positions not because they hoped to recover their initial expense with the salaries; rather, they regarded these positions as entry to some other lucrative gains, legal or otherwise.

## Ruling a Colony

Fray Domingo de Salazar, O.P., the first bishop of the Philippines, arrived in Manila on 17 September 1581. Contrary winds had stopped his boat from negotiating the narrow San Bernardino Strait between Sorsogon and Samar, before sailing north to Cavite. After a while, the bishop, with the Franciscan and Jesuit missionaries, went ashore and hiked from what is now Albay to Laguna, where they took a boat down the Pasig River to Manila.

Though long and tiring, the overland route gave the bishop first-hand knowledge of the sufferings in the new colony after ten years of Spanish colonization. A friar's report explained why:

> This is how the land is pacified. A captain with soldiers and interpreters goes to a settlement. . . . They tell the people if they want to be friends with the Spaniards they must pay the tribute at once. If the people say yes, they stop to work out what each man must give. . . . Sometimes the people refuse to give what is asked; then they sack the settlement. . . . The natives say they do not want the friendship of the Spaniards or . . . build fortifications to defend themselves. Those who do this are killed or made prisoners, and their houses plundered and burned.

Even if exaggerated, the report shows that people were abused, and some of them tried to resist. A brave man from Cainta (of the present province of Rizal), for example, climbed up a coconut tree after a skirmish with the Spaniards and shouted, "Spaniards, what did our fathers do to you, or what debt did they owe you?" But superior weapons wore down native resistance, and the Spaniards conquered the country.

By 1580, rice, if it could still be found, cost thrice its price in 1570. In 1570, twelve to sixteen chickens cost 0.50 pesos; ten years later, the same amount bought only four. A large pig in 1570 cost 0.60 pesos; in 1580, a small pig was priced at 4 pesos, medium-sized at 5 pesos, and a large one at 6 pesos. Prices had increased, and the people were in need of everything.

Worse, menfolk were taken to fight with the Spanish soldiers. For example, about 1,000 were recruited from a town in Pampanga, and many failed to return. Those who did were either too sick or too exhausted to work their farms. Harvests were left to rot, crops were not planted, and people died of hunger.

Missionaries naturally condemned this. They charged the Spanish colonists with the sin of injustice, unforgivable in confession unless they returned what they had stolen. The cruel acts of the Spanish conquistadores blocked the very conquest and Christianization of the islands.

It has been mentioned that such cruelty was due to hunger. There was not enough rice even for the natives themselves, so that when the European strangers swooped down on the land, they mercilessly left the people with even less.

In the Spanish tradition, a conquered land was divided into *encomiendas* or sectors of land, together with the inhabitants, who were entrusted (in Spanish, *encomendar* is "to entrust") to the encomendero as a reward for his service to the crown. But the latter was obliged to resettle the people in a permanent community, provide them a just government and protection from their enemies, and teach them the Christian doctrine. In return for these tasks by which the encomendero "discharged the royal conscience," he could collect the tribute, and have several men working to plant crops, fell logs, keep watch over the townhall at night, serve as mail runners or oarsmen for the officials, etc.

Unfortunately in the beginning, there was no uniform rate for the tribute, and laws for the encomienda were unclear. Thus, hungry themselves, the Spaniards demanded and grabbed all they could. Unable to defend themselves, the people packed off and fled to the mountains.

It was a desperate dilemma. The conquered tribes who lived in the settlement or *reducción* were sorely harassed. Those who fled to the mountains *(remontados)* soon gave up the Christian faith.

As a solution, Bishop Salazar convoked what is now called the First Synod of Manila late in 1582. Invited were the superiors of the religious orders and a number of the leading priests, plus some prominent colonists who had had some experience in the Philippines.

Immediately before the synod formally opened, the fathers condemned slavery. Both king and pope had declared all men were free, and they, too, were forbidding the practice by the Spanish colonists, on pain of denial of sacramental absolution, and by the natives on pain of being refused Christian baptism, or, if already baptized, the sacraments. Those who wanted to rectify their marriage before the church had to promise at least in writing that they would free their slaves.

The synod next faced a more serious problem: What right did Spain have to rule the Philippines? One of the Augustinians had said that "none among all these islands have come into power of the Spaniards with just title." Others answered that Spain had a duty to rule the Philippines because of her *delegated* authority from the pope. Since the latter alone could not spread the Christian Gospel throughout the world, he delegated rulers to perform the task in his name. This task could be carried out if Spain assumed temporal control also of the archipelago. Who would protect the missionaries or their future converts? Where would church expenses come from, the money to shelter or feed the missionaries? Would Christianity in the Philippines grow peacefully if the Spanish government did not "guard" the islands? Spain, then, had a right to colonize the Philippines in order to create a situation favorable for Christianity.

But if the Spaniards could rightly rule the Philippines, what was the best form of government for the colony? The synod agreed that all the colonial officials exercised authority only in the king's name. Their first duty was to see that all were treated justly. They were expected to know the king's laws, and they had to oversee subordinate officials in the exercise of royal justice. For the biggest problem in the fledgling colony was abusive officials unconcerned with the welfare of the people, "exploiting them, beating them, forcing them to work against their will or without pay, 'requisitioning' their meager store of food, confiscating their boats, ravishing their wives and daughters, and inflicting many other injuries upon them."

The fathers also declared that the encomienda was granted, "not so much to reward the encomendero . . . as to discharge the conscience of the King with reference to the natives of the encomienda." In other words, ideally the encomendero was appointed to perform the king's duties, such as maintaining peace and order, providing means of livelihood, and protecting the people from their enemies. He neither owned the encomienda, nor did he rule the people for his own good.

The synod also agreed that native-born leaders should share in the responsibilities of the colonial government. Local magistrates should be elected by the people. Peace and order in the towns and court cases up to 200 pesos should be within the competence of local magistrates.

Other matters pertaining to the good of the colony were settled. Lists of "duties" were made for the soldiers, Chinese traders, army and navy officers, widows, etc. The lists were intended as a guide for colonial society.

The synod closed on a hopeful note. At least in *theory*, it was clear how the Philippines should be ruled. An *ideal* colonial system had been drawn up. For one and all, there was a clear reminder of what, as Christians, they should do for the Philippines. Furthermore, a clear definition was also made of what consisted robbery of a helpless people.

## Suggestions for Further Reading

*(Complete information on recommended readings appears in the bibliography at the end of the book.)*

Cushner, Nicholas P., *Spain in the Philippines;* Phelan, John L., *The Hispanization of the Philippines: Spanish aims and Filipino responses, 1565–1700;* Scott, William H., "Class structure in the unhispanized Philippines," *PS* 27; Scott, William H., "Filipino class structure in the sixteenth century," *PS* 28.

# 4

## MEETING OF CULTURES

### The Missionary's Role

When he left Mexico in 1564, Legazpi carried instructions to set up only a trading post *(factoría)*, without attempting to impose Spanish rule. As worded, part of his duty was

> to bring to the inhabitants of those places our Holy Catholic Faith and to discover the return route to this New Spain . . . through trade and barter and through other legitimate ways, which with a clear conscience should be carried on to bring back some spices and some of the wealth found in those places.

But, after Urdaneta's return voyage linked the new colony to the home government, the crown decided to conquer the Philippines. Legazpi received the title "governor general" of the future colony, with political authority, not only over the island of Cebu, but also over the "other settlements which you or any other person whatever may hereafter seek in the island." He was also ordered to divide and entrust (in Spanish, *encomendar*) lands to deserving Spaniards.

In other words, the colonization of the Philippines was through the encomienda. This did not mean giving lands away; rather, in the king's name, the people were introduced to Spanish law and the Christian faith. When the people were ready, the encomendero was supposed to summon the missionary to baptize them.

In this way, the encomenderos would be "discharging the royal conscience," or fulfilling for the king his duty to spread the Christian Gospel. For this reason, almost every boat sailing to the Philippines had, as passengers, both royal officials and missionaries.

Spanish law decreed that the Spanish language was to be taught in all the colonies of Spain. But soon experience taught the missionaries it was easier for them to learn the indigenous tongues than for entire villages to learn Spanish. Thus it was decided that Christianity would be preached in the people's idioms. Hence, in order to preach successfully, the missionaries had to learn the idioms spoken in the missions. That is why the missionaries were the first to compose the first grammars and dictionaries of the Philippine tongues.

Some important Christian mysteries, however, could not be expressed in any local word, and the missionaries used Spanish terms instead. For example, instead of the Tagalog *Bathala*, they introduced the Spanish word *Dios* to avoid confusion: The people also believed in one supreme god but also worshiped several lesser gods. This was not the Christian idea of a unique, exclusive God, and the missionaries wanted the people to forget the old gods.

In accustoming the people to the Spanish life-style, other Spanish words were also introduced. To till the land, they were taught how to use the plow or *araro* (Spanish *arado*); or build houses with windows, *ventanas* (today *bintana* in Pilipino).

Settlements were planned around a square plaza. On one side was the church, opposite it was the townhall *(tribunal)*, on the third side the school, and on the fourth the houses of the leading persons of the community. Streets *(calles)* were opened at right angles to one another, along which houses were built in a line. Finally, the people began to eat with the *cuchara*, wear shoes (*sapatos* from *zapatos*), etc.

Improved agricultural techniques also meant new plants and animals. The horse and the cow, for example, were introduced through China. From Mexico the missionaries brought cacao which was made into chocolate, sugar cane which was sold as *panocha* or cakes of brown sugar, papaya, peanuts whose original name was *cacahuates,* tomatoes, and other plants that have since become acclimatized here.

More importantly, perhaps, the people were taught how to set aside part of the harvest for future planting, assuring a steady food supply without having to wander from place to place to look for it.

And while waiting for the crops to ripen, the people had the free time to learn the *Doctrina Cristiana* or catechism. They learned to pray at different times during the day; the Angelus, for example, was recited at sunrise, noon, sundown, and at about eight o'clock at night, when the church bell ringer invited the people to pray for the souls in purgatory. On Sundays, or feast days, they had special religious functions.

Thus, people soon adjusted to a regular routine or time schedule. Their waking hours were divided into prayer, work, rest, and recreation; the week was set off by Sunday Mass and other obligations; and the year by the celebration of Easter, Christmas, and their patron saint's day.

The coming, then, of Spanish missionaries enriched indigenous society. The Christian catechism could not have been learned had the people not been taught basic learning skills, such as reading, writing, and memorizing. And because the missionaries used the Roman alphabet instead of the prehispanic script, the Philippines came to share in the Greco-Roman tradition of culture and learning. How successfully the missionaries educated the people can be seen from the words of the midnineteenth-century French traveler, Jean Mallat, who wrote that there were more people who were literate in the Philippines than in Europe!

## Initial Changes

Manila was organized just like the other Spanish colonial cities in South America. The Filipinos were vassals of the crown, and they were instructed in the Christian faith. They were promised protection and good government, but they also had certain obligations to fulfill.

On 3 June 1572, Legazpi made Manila the seat of the "New Kingdom of Castile." On the 24th, the first city officials were appointed: two *alcaldes ordinarios*, one alguacil mayor, twelve *regidores*, and one *escribano de cabildo*. Finally, on the 28th, "in the name of most Holy Trinity, Father, Son, and Holy Spirit, in the presence of His Illustrious Lordship Miguel López de Legazpi and Hernando Riquel, his *Escribano mayor de gobierno*," the first city ordinances and instructions were promulgated. All the new officials took the oath to observe them.

Manila was now a Spanish city. But that Manila is not the Manila of today, now is it to be confused with the prehispanic settlement of Maynilad, north of the Pasig where the native's lived. It was that city "within the walls" of Intramuros. And that Spanish city was made the center of operations for the conquest of the rest of the islands, as well as the outpost for the projected China trade.

After the pacification of the Laguna lake area, Juan de Salcedo conquered in succession Pampanga, Pangasinan, and the Ilocos. He then proceeded down the eastern coast of Luzon until the present Quezon province. From there, he crossed the mountains, reaching Manila just after Legazpi, his grandfather, had died on 20 August 1572.

Guido de Lavezaris succeeded as governor of the Philippines. He was the first *regidor* (officer in charge) of the Spanish city of Santísimo Nombre de Jesús on the island of Cebu. This should not be confused with Sugbu, the prehispanic port. For the Spaniards did not destroy native settlements but instead founded nearby "cities" for the Spanish crown. In time, the two sectors merged into one.

As governor general in Manila, Lavezaris had to defend the colony against the Chinese corsair, Limahong, who appeared in Manila Bay on 29 November 1574. Native auxiliaries fought alongside the Spaniards, but others renounced their new allegiance. Through the diplomacy of an Augustinian missionary, however, many were won back and helped fight against the Chinese. Juan de Salcedo arrived from the north just in time to strengthen the defenses. Limahong retreated to Pangasinan, where he managed to slip through the Spanish-Filipino blockade and was heard of no more.

Francisco de Sande arrived in 1575 as the next governor of the Philippines. He continued the pacification of the country. Pedro de Chávez was sent to win Camarines and found a new Spanish city there, Nueva Cáceres. In 1577, the Franciscan missionaries arrived and three years later, Esteban Rodríguez de Figueroa received royal authorization to pacify Mindanao and Sulu. In 1581, the first bishop of the Philippines, Fray Domingo de Salazar, arrived. With him came the first Jesuits to the Philippines.

The pacification of the archipelago continued. Juan Pablo de Carrión explored the still unopened province of Cagayan, from where he dislodged a Japanese community. To consolidate Spanish hold of the area, Carrión left there a military detachment and founded the city of Nueva Segovia. At this time, Arévalo in Panay island was also founded.

Santiago de Vera arrived in 1584 as governor of the Philippines. He strongly suggested the establishment of the audiencia to check abuses by government personnel, although the colonial treasury could hardly pay for the salaries of its members or oidores.

During his term, Agustín de Legazpi, a gobernadorcillo in Tondo, was convicted of misconduct in office. Embarrassed and feeling degraded, he soon came to hate the Spaniards. He planned to overthrow the government. When a Japanese trading fleet arrived in Manila, he contacted its captain for aid and arms. Unfortunately for him, someone leaked the news to the government and the expected reenforcements from Japan did not materialize. The plotters were easily rounded up. Eight of the thirty leaders were executed, the rest were either exiled to Mexico or penalized with lighter sentences.

Manila in the sixteenth century, honored with the high-sounding title of "Noble and Ever Loyal City," was still a city of nipa, bamboo, or wooden structures. In 1583, during the funeral rites of Governor Gonzalo Ronquillo de Peñalosa, it burned down completely in a few hours. To avoid similar disasters, the city ordained that only stone structures would be approved for construction.

Stone masonry or bricklaying was unknown, but luckily, the first Jesuit superior in the Philippines, Fr. Antonio Sedeño, knew something about the art. He taught the Filipinos masonry and how to cut stone. Subsequently, he was commissioned to build the first concrete fort in the islands, today Fort Santiago in Intramuros, Manila. The same priest also taught Chinese artists to produce western religious art to decorate the first churches in the Philippines. He had introduced the mulberry tree and silkworms to start a silk weaving industry, but Philippine weather conditions neutralized his efforts.

In 1590, twenty years after Legazpi had founded the Spanish city of Manila, the Philippine population was estimated at 667,000, or a total of 166,903 tributes collected from 31 royal encomiendas, or those whose tributes belonged exclusively to the government, and 236 private encomiendas, or those whose tributes were collected by encomenderos who gave only a part to the government.

Though notoriously inaccurate, tribute lists (*padrones*) offer a good summary of Philippine society. At the top were the *principales*: incumbent and past gobernadorcillos or barangay heads, their wives, and oldest sons. They neither paid the tribute nor took turns at the polo or yearly public service of forty days (reduced to fifteen days in 1885). Below them were the married tribute payers. Each full tribute was 1 peso or 8 *reales* (later increased to 10, then 12), paid in three installments. The third group were the widowers and unmarried males between eighteen and sixty years of age, who paid a half-tribute. Then came the exemptees, those below eighteen and above sixty years of age, the sick, those employed in the church (*fiscal* or caretaker and priest's substitute, *cantores*, *sacristanes*). We next have two lists of the young: those allowed to receive holy communion, besides going merely to confession (*comulgantes*); the younger ones who were obliged to go to confession but were not old enough to receive holy communion (*solo confesión*). Finally, there was the group of *niños de pecho*, generally children below seven years of age. Boys were listed separately from the girls. In Pangasinan, some girls volunteered to be listed among the older girls to avoid the weekly turn to wash church linen, or pound rice for the parish priest.

Official warnings that the polo was not meant for the personal service of government or church officials were frequent. This means abuses were rampant, and the government tried in vain to prevent them. The law also provided that the polistas were to be given food rations, paid a daily wage, and not to be taken to distant work sites, etc. But the colonial treasury was almost always empty. And so, the Manila government requisitioned food rations (*bandalas*) from specific towns and borrowed funds from local treasuries. Soon the central government was indebted, and when the people could no longer suffer it, they rose in arms. Until Bonifacio's uprising in 1896, what traditional history calls revolutions are better called uprisings or mutinies with hardly a political motive behind them, such as independence. They were, rather, violent reactions against extremely unbearable socioeconomic conditions.

## Early Economic Changes

The Spaniards thought that the Philippines was rich. This impression came from the first tributes from Ilocos and Pangasinan totaling the huge sum of 109,500 pesos. And in 1587, an English buccaneer sacked an Ilocos town and sailed away richer by 30,000 pesos.

Actually, these were isolated instances. Gold could indeed be found in the Philippines, but, except for the little the Igorots in the present Mountain Province mined, it stayed unexploited.

There were, however, indigenous industries by which people earned a living. The arrival of the Spaniards practically killed these, but a few managed to survive in the provinces. The Jesuit missionary, Francisco Alcina who went to the Visayas in 1635, wrote that the most respected trade was that of the smith who made bolos, knives, axes, and other tools used for the *kaingin* style of farming. The smith also fashioned fighting weapons, both of iron and wood hardened by fire.

Another native occupation was tailoring. The people generally wove their own cloth and sewed their own clothes. In time, European styles were followed. The women were traditionally the weavers of cloth, probably of fibers such as abaca and *piña* and even cotton, which was not unknown in Ilocos and Pangasinan. In fact, one of the products made famous abroad by the galleon trade was the thick Ilocano cotton cloth which could also be used as a sail. Abaca fibers produced a coarse cloth, often used for skirts, called *bacacay* in Visayan, or in Tagalog *pinukpok*, while cotton was used not only for clothing but also for blankets.

While most women were engaged with the needle and the weaving loom, men worked as carpenters. They made household furniture, like tables and benches, besides wooden plates, wooden trays, and wooden pans. Besides these, the carpenters built their own houses and made rattan mats and baskets for storing rice. Because their only tool for various operations was the native bolo, the Spaniards never ceased to wonder at their skill in using it.

A curious occupation among the Filipinos was the barber's. Strictly speaking, there was neither a barber nor a barber shop. The wife cut her husband's hair, the husband cut his wife's. No razor or comb was used. But hair was trimmed "with great facility with only a *najita* of cane . . . which they put under the scissors . . . very evenly and well without the necessity of other instruments," according to Father Alcina.

When the Spaniards came, the people were grouped in barangays under a datu. They lived on land that all the barangay members helped to cultivate. No one claimed any parcel of territory as private property.

Except for weapons, hunting tools, and personal adornments, the prehispanic islanders did not recognize private ownership. There was plenty of land for everyone, and the cultivated area was limited only by the number of workers available and the threat of a neighboring tribe.

By right of conquest, the Spanish crown claimed all the lands, and freed the people from their datus—but made them vassals of the king. Their former leaders took on the positions of gobernadorcillos or barangay heads, for which they received land as their private property. However, although the gobernadorcillos and barangay heads preserved their political leadership, they lost followers who used to fight their battles and till the land for them. They had lost the economic basis for their traditional leadership.

It was not easy to accept the new system. In 1589, Magat Salamat and a few other gobernadorcillos tried to revolt during the term of Governor Santiago de Vera. But the plot was discovered and they paid for their daring.

Soon, deprived of workers to till their lands, most of the landowning gobernadorcillos and barangay heads sold their property. Thus, instead of political leaders owning lands, even if honored as the principalia, they soon were added to the number of landless *indios*, as the Filipinos were then called by the Spaniards.

What about the former subjects freed from the authority of the datus? They had no property to begin with, and the new system did not change their economic situation. They remained a propertyless and poor.

Thus, right from the start, the small landowning elite was separated from the more populous but poor Filipinos. Philippine society was divided between the few rich and the numerous poor. We shall see more of this later.

## Suggestions for Further Reading

*(Complete information on recommended readings appears in the bibliography at the end of the book.)*

Aduarte, Diego, "History of the Dominican province of the holy rosary," in *BR* 30–32; "The Augustinian Recollects," in *BR* 28; Chirino, Pedro, "Relation of the Philippines Islands," in *BR* 12–13; Colin, Francisco, "Jesuit missions in 1656," in *BR* 28; "Early Franciscan missions," in *BR* 35; Llorente, Ana María M., *A blending of cultures: The Batanes, 1686–1898;* Medina, Juan de, "History of the Augustinian order in the Philippines," in *BR* 23–24; Murillo Velarde, Pedro, "Jesuit missions in the seventeenth century," in *BR* 45.

# 5

## INITIAL COLONIAL PROBLEMS

### The Chinese

Right from the beginning, the increasing number of Chinese arriving in Manila every year worried the Spaniards. But long before the latter's arrival, Chinese merchants had already been trading with the native islanders. Two or three junks usually went yearly to Sulu for pearls, to Cebu for cotton, and to Manila for slaves. The Chinese also came to exploit the gold in Paracale, Camarines Norte, or the copper in Botolan, Zambales.

While the traders sailed back to China, others stayed permanently. Soon, there were more Chinese than Spaniards in the Philippines. In 1570, for example, there were only 40 Chinese in Manila, but in 1603, about thirty years later, their number had grown to an estimated 25,000.

This alarmed the authorities, who wanted to expel all of the Chinese. Later, the authorities decided to confine them in special residential sectors called *Parián* in Manila, Cebu, and other Spanish cities. Some Manila residents, however, employed them as cobblers, gardeners, drivers of their carrozas, cooks, etc., preferring them to the indios, described as "naturally lazy." Besides, the missionaries wanted them around to christianize them. They hoped the baptized Chinese in the Philippines would serve to convert the millions in the Chinese mainland.

There was, then, no agreement regarding the Chinese. In the beginning, the Spaniards considered the Philippines only as a jumping board to either conquer or Christianize China. The Manila government, however, convinced the king that with the millions of pagans in the Philippines the missionaries had enough to occupy them without thinking of China. The king, therefore, forbade the missionaries from leaving the Philippines. But meanwhile, Spanish prejudice against the Chinese hardened.

And yet, the first meeting between the two races had been friendly. On his way to Manila in 1571, Legazpi saved some Chinese traders from Muslim pirates and restored their goods to them. The next year, Chinese junks arrived in Manila to sell food and Oriental goods. At that time, the colony was suffering from a shortage of rations, and their arrival saved the situation. More importantly, the Oriental goods they had brought were reshipped to Mexico where they fetched high prices.

Soon a pattern was set: Chinese and Oriental goods were brought to Manila aboard Chinese junks, transferred to Spanish boats or galleons, and brought to Mexico where they earned a handsome profit. The galleon trade had begun, to continue for two-and-a-half centuries until 1815, when the last galleon left Acapulco for Manila.

On 29 November 1574, a fleet of sixty-two to seventy sail and a complement of 3,000 fighters, besides 1,500 women, artisans, and medical practitioners, suddenly loomed off the western horizon of Manila Bay. The Chinese corsair, Limahong, had just escaped after ravaging a city on the southern China coast, and wanted more.

Near Luzon, he came upon a boat Juan de Salcedo had sent to look for rations. The pirate killed all its passengers, except the pilot whom he forced to serve as a guide. Stopping off Mariveles, Limahong sent ahead an assault force of 400 men. He had learned there were not more than twenty Spaniards in the city, and on the night of 28 November, a Japanese ally was already sailing into Manila Bay. But a storm sank three of the invading boats. The others reached Parañaque, south of Manila, and at sunrise, landed; and Limahong's forces marched in good order toward the city (of Intramuros). Some people hurried to warn the field marshall of Manila, Martín de Goyti. But he paid no attention, thinking it was another of those alarms by the "fearful" indios. Before he knew it, the Chinese were upon him. Martín de Goyti was cut down in the ensuing skirmish.

Juan de Salcedo was in Ilocos at this time, but noting the strange fleet sailing down the west coast of Luzon, he had correctly guessed its aggressive intent. Rushing south to the city, he arrived just in time to fight off the Chinese, who escaped to Pangasinan. Somehow, Limahong and his men slipped away and sailed up the Cagayan River in northwestern Luzon. Although the Spaniards mounted a blockade, Limahong succeeded in evading capture.

The royal court made the necessary investigations; but with no clear proof of neglect, everyone was exonerated. The incident, however, was not lost on the Spaniards who never forgot that the Chinese could easily swoop down and take the Philippines from them. Fear deepened prejudice.

A second incident further explains Spanish animosity for the Chinese colony. Tiongeng, a Chinese cabinet maker, reported there was a mountain of gold and silver in "Keit." Three mandarins subsequently arrived in Manila in May 1603. The governor general received them, but with misgivings. Allowed in the Parián, the mandarins began to administer justice. This confirmed fears that the mandarins' visit was the prelude to invasion. Keit was most probably Cavite, where the galleons bringing silver from Mexico docked. Tiongeng was escorted back to China, but defense works were set up.

Exaggerated rumors spread around, Tagalog hotheads provoked the Chinese. On the eve of 4 October 1603, the rumored uprising began. But well-organized government troops with Filipino auxiliaries overpowered the Chinese, about 15,000 of whom died.

Several times, in 1639, 1662, 1686, 1762, and 1819, the Chinese were again victimized. Sometimes they were provoked to strike the first blow, and Spanish retaliation was merciless.

In 1644, the Manchu Tartars dethroned the Ming dynasty in China. By and large, the Chinese accepted the new rulers, also known as the Ts'ing dynasty. But Koxinga (also "Tching-tching-cong") assumed the military leadership of those who still favored the old emperor. In a decisive battle, he lost to the Ts'ing and fled to Amuy, an island close to Formosa. He soon had many followers, for whom he had to look for a homeland. He thought of Formosa and the Philippines.

After a ten-month blockade, he dislodged the Dutch from Formosa who had conquered the island from the Spaniards twenty years previously in 1642. His next objective was the Philippines, and in May 1662, he sent a dire warning that the "small Spanish kingdom" would be forgiven their crimes if they recognized his authority. Otherwise, his forces would immediately raze "your fortifications, dams, cities, and depots, . . . pulverize the stones themselves even if later you ask pardon and pay tributes in recognition; but in vain, it will be too late."

The Manila government tried to keep everything secret. But defense preparations told everyone something was afoot. Again, before something worse befell them, the Chinese decided to land the first blow. As before, unfortunately, they were no match for the better organized government forces and native auxiliaries.

One of the more serious effects of this incident was the governor general's decision, as a precaution, to recall to Manila all the military and naval garrisons from the south: Calamianes in Palawan, Iligan and Zamboanga in Mindanao, and Ternate in the spice islands. As feared, the removal of the southern military units in 1663 left the seas unguarded, and the Moros resumed their piratical raids with more ferocity than ever.

As for the Chinese, they were eventually allowed to stay. They married Filipino women. And soon a new racial type appeared, the Chinese mestizo, culturally Filipino, but externally Chinese—with fair skin and Oriental eyes. But more than just externally: the mestizo apparently inherited a generous share of their ancestors' skills as well as discipline and habits of hard work. And, in time, this progeny influenced Philippine history. Their names are familiar: Rizal, Aguinaldo, San Lorenzo Ruiz, Mother Ignacia del Espíritu Santo, Osmeña, etc. Hardly anyone today in the Philippines is without Chinese admixture. Perhaps the greatest foreign element in Filipino blood is Chinese.

## The Moro Raids

When the Spaniards arrived in 1565, the Muslims in southwestern Mindanao and Sulu were already socially organized. The lowest among them were the slaves, mostly captives or their descendants. Over these were the *tuan*, equivalent to the Tagalog timawa. The ruling class, the "strong men," were the *orongkaia*. A fourth class was the fighting class of princes or warlords. They enjoyed immense power in religious and political issues.

The waters of Sulu produced some pearl, but not enough. Neither did the fertile Maguindanao plain provide enough rice or sago. The people were forced to look for other sources of income. Skilled boatmen, they soon were brave sailors engaged in daring raids in the Visayas and farther north and south, to supply the slave markets of Southeast Asia. Then the Spaniards came, threatening their economy. This led to war.

In 1578, Esteban Rodríguez de Figueroa led an expedition to Sulu. But Raja Pangiran of Sulu refused his offer of friendship and chose to fight instead. The battle was short and swift. On 14 June, the raja came to terms with the victor, acknowledging "himself and his descendants vassals of His Majesty, Don Philipe, King of Castile and Leon." In token of his fealty and vassalage, he gave twelve pearls and thirty-five gold *taels* "in his name and that of his subjects the islands of Joló, Tagima, Samboangan, Kawit, and Tawi-Tawi, these being his dominions." Figueroa then sailed to Maguindanao; but here the rajas fled, avoiding peaceful talks with the Spaniards awaiting them offshore. When supplies ran low, the Spanish forces went away. Pangiran in Sulu forgot all about them.

Twenty years later, in 1595, Figueroa reappeared near the fortification of Buayan, the Maguindanao stronghold. The Spaniard sent a reconnoitering unit ashore; but, impatient, landed himself. At a turn of the grassy path, a hidden Muslim raised his kampilan, but the quicker Figueroa cut his man down. He had not gone a few more steps forward when a second kampilan flashed in the air. This time the blade found its mark. Figueroa never recovered consciousness and died the next day.

The Spaniards waited, but discouraged and surprised at Buayan's strength, they persuaded Juan de la Jara, the next commanding officer, to sail away. The first attempt to conquer the Maguindanao Muslims, therefore, had failed. Instead it aroused Muslim ire, and from 1599 onward, they sailed their marauding speedy vintas north to the Visayas and Luzon. In 1602, one group led by Siroman and Raja Mura attacked Calamianes and Mindoro, taking about 700 captives; a second group led by Raja Buisan ravaged the ports of Balayan and Calilayan in Batangas.

The coastal missions in the Visayas and Luzon were open prey. And besides attacking, the Muslim raiders tried to undermine Spanish authority and convince the people to renounce their faith and their oath of loyalty to the crown.

The missionaries, left to themselves, arranged a system of evacuation to the hinterlands when hostile vintas appeared. They built stone watchtowers along the shore, some of which are still standing.

Once, the system failed and too late to hide himself after sheltering a slow-footed Christian in Leyte, the Jesuit Fr. Melchor Hurtado was captured. He was well treated and even shared the same food as Sirongan and the other datus. He learned enough Moro to converse with his captors in their own tongue about the differences between Christianity and Islam. He was later ransomed, together with other Christian captives.

The trouble was no adequate defense was set up by the government. The vintas, practically flying before the wind, easily outmaneuvered the bulky Spanish craft. And the raids continued, until garrisons were set up, one in Caraga in eastern Mindanao, the other in Zamboanga.

The strategy worked, for Spanish cannons picked off the vintas on their way home from their raids. Besides, with the garrisons, Jesuit missionaries soon had a base of operations from which to evangelize the surrounding areas.

Then, as mentioned, Governor Manrique de Lara recalled all the Spanish garrisons in southern Philippines. In May 1662, a Chinese delegation led by the Dominican Fray Vittorino Ricci delivered a message from Tching-tching-cong (Koxinga), who had just driven the Dutch from Formosa, and was intending to do the same to the Spaniards in the Philippines. Unless tribute was paid him, he threatened to conquer Manila.

Manrique was not daunted and immediately put up the defenses. He concentrated all the Spanish forces in Manila, abandoning Caraga and Zamboanga. As for the Sulus and Maguindanaos, they lost no time in occupying Zamboanga. Koxinga never made good his boast. He died. But the garrisons were not returned, and the raids resumed.

# European Politics and the Philippines

When Philip II ascended the Spanish throne, Belgium, Holland, and Luxembourg belonged to his kingdom. In 1581, they won independence as the United Dutch Provinces. Philip, who was also king of Portugal, closed the port of Lisbon to Dutch trading. To continue their eastern trade, the Dutch organized the United East India Company. By 1600, they sought to break the Hispano-Lusitanian control of Manila, which was the key to the spice islands. Thus, early in the seventeenth century, Spain had to face a third problem: the Dutch menace.

The Dutch knew the Philippines was poor, and they did not agree among themselves about conquering it. But they wanted the Mexican silver the galleons were bringing every year to Manila. They also wanted to divert the Chinese traders to the Dutch-controlled islands south of the Philippines and to cut off the China-Manila trade. To do so, they tried blockading Manila, and one of their naval commanders urged that

> the best and only means of . . . making ourselves masters of the Moluccas is in my opinion to dispatch a fleet and armada directly to the Philippines in order to attack the Spaniards there and overpower all the places and strongholds it may be possible to conquer.

In 1600, Oliver van Noort steered his two ships close to Manila, but the Spaniards put up a fight. Though one Spanish vessel sank, van Noort had to flee to Borneo.

Several more times, especially in 1610, 1617, and 1625, the Dutch attacked the Philippines. In 1610, the Dutch lost not only three ships but also their captain, Francois Wittert. Seven years later, the Dutch again lost three out of nine ships, although they also damaged some Spanish ships. Finally, in 1625, an outnumbered Spanish contingent of only seven ships faced and routed a bigger Dutch fleet.

In all these battles known in Philippine history as the Battles of Playa Honda, the Spaniards worsted their enemies, a fact attributed to the prayers of the Mother of God. For example, when there were no iron cables with which to lash Spanish guns aboard the ships, a substitute was found in carabao hides. Another time, when a Dutch vessel was about to capture an incoming galleon, night fell and in the dark, the Spanish ship slipped away. In thanksgiving for victory, therefore, every year since the Manileños have celebrated the feast of Our Lady of the Rosary with special pomp. Until now, on 7 October each year, the feast popularly known as La Naval, is celebrated solemnly.

But what did the Dutch accomplish? They did lessen Chinese shipping to Manila, but fearing a "loss of name" before the Chinese, they stopped harassing Spanish galleons and concentrated their efforts around Malacca and the Moluccas Islands.

In 1641, Malacca fell, and although it became a convenient Dutch base of operations, the Dutch still failed to completely cripple the Manila-Acapulco trade. From 1646 to 1647, they were at the Embocadero, or the strait between Sorsogon and Samar, waiting to ambush galleons entering from the Pacific. But after a month, when no galleon appeared and their supplies began to run low, they sailed away. But the Spaniards gave pursuit and, again, bested them.

Finally, in 1648, Dutch hostilities against the Philippines ended. In Europe, the warring parties signed the Treaty of Münster. Article 5 provided that the Dutch were to stay out of Philippine waters, while the Spaniards were to keep away from Batavia (today Jakarta in Indonesia). As with the treaties of that period, it was a dead letter, because undercover trade went on as before.

All this fighting naturally affected the natives. They were auxiliary fighters or crewmen for the Spaniards, workers in the navy yards, or cutters of forest timber for the Spanish ships. The law that they should be paid for their labor was hardly enforced. In 1619, expenses for one month totaled about forty reales, but work gangs received only eight! To cover up the deficit, the government requisitioned both food (called *bandala*) and funds from the towns, a levy frequently left unpaid or forgotten.

And so the government fell into heavy debt. In 1617, it owed the towns of Antipolo, Taytay, San Miguel, and Indang the amount of 8,083 pesos for unpaid bandalas and 6,643 pesos for debts to pay for workers' wages.

When the people could no longer stand it, they mutinied. In 1649, for example, Governor Fajardo recruited labor gangs from the Visayas, instead of from Luzon. The number needed was not excessive, only one laborer from each village. But the shipyard in Cavite was too far from home. Resentment found a leader in Sumuroy, the garrison leader in Palapag, Samar. The uprising soon spread throughout the Visayas, Bicol, and Camiguin off northern Mindanao. The rebels were soon subdued, but not before some Jesuit missionaries and Spaniards had lost their lives.

In 1660, the Pampangos rose in revolt. Again, it was because they had not been paid for their work. The revolt was particularly dangerous because the province was prosperous and the Pampangos, invariably serving as Spanish auxiliaries, were familiar with Spanish military tactics. The governor acted fast. He split the province in two by occupying Arayat town, while securing the southern half of the province. Then he invited leaders of the northern provinces of Pangasinan and Ilocos to a parley in Manila. But as soon as the governor felt militarily secure, he stopped negotiations and executed the rebel leaders. Another abrupt end to another uprising.

There were other uprisings, but the government invariably quashed them. They were individual, local movements, for the people were not yet united into a nation. But they show that the colonial government in the Philippines did not remain unaffected by political developments in Europe or by those closer in Asia.

### Suggestions for Further Reading

*(Complete information on recommended readings appears in the bibliography at the end of the book.)*

Díaz-Trechuelo, María Lourdes, "The economic background," in Félix, Alfonso, Jr., *The Chinese in the Philippines*, vol. 2; Ileto, Reynaldo C., *Magindanao, 1860–1888: The career of Datu Uto of Buayan*; Majul, César Adib, *Muslims in the Philippines*; Mallari, Francisco R., *Ibalon under storm and siege: Essays on Bicol history, 1565–1860*; Wickberg, Edgar, *The Chinese in Philippine life*.

# 6

## THE FARTHEST SPANISH COLONY

### Patronato Real

In 1582, Bishop Salazar invited the superiors of the missionaries and some experienced colonial leaders to a synod in Manila to remedy the problems of the new colony. They concluded that the root of the problems was corruption among royal officials. Should these officials, they asked, be removed? Why were native leaders deposed? Should they be restored and the Spaniards made to leave the country?

Not necessarily, Bishop Salazar explained. King Philip II of Spain exercised authority over his kingdoms both as a "natural" and a "supernatural" sovereign. A natural sovereign was one who inherited the crown, was voted to receive it, or won it in a just war. None of these conditions was true in King Philip's case, but he justly ruled the Philippines by virtue of the supernatural jurisdiction entrusted to him by the pope. The latter could not preach the Gospel all over the world by himself and needed the help of others.

Neither was rebellion against bad officials justifiable for this was to exchange one evil for another!

The remedy lay in the royal conscience. The king, under pain of sin, should appoint only good officials. If, despite precautions, the appointees turned out to be corrupt and dishonest, the king should depose and punish them.

The Philippines, then, needed rulers who would help above all to plant Christianity in the islands. In other words, like in South America, Spain ruled the Philippines in order to establish the church.

This was the *Patronato real de Indias*, the set of privileges called *regalias* enjoyed by the Spanish crown, chief of which was being able to nominate persons to vacancies in the church.

When a bishop or a priest was needed, a *terna* or list of three names was submitted from which the king chose one to recommend to the pope, for the post of bishop or parish priest. In the colonies, the crown built the churches and furnished them with sacred vessels, altar vestments, books, bells, holy images, etc. Expenses in the missions, like Mass wine, flour for the hosts for consecration, wax for the candles, etc. would also be shouldered by the royal treasury. Each missionary was granted a yearly stipend of 100 pesos, plus 100 *fanegas* of rice. In return, the crown collected the tribute and the tithe.

But as the years passed, the government claimed more privileges and subtly *controlled*, instead of just helped the church. It argued that since it was responsible for the church, it should be allowed to exercise authority over it. Responsibility implied authority. Yes, but how much authority?

The pope explained that royal privileges did not include spiritual authority. For example, the Spanish crown could collect church offerings, or tithes, provided that part of this money would be used to satisfy the material needs of the church.

But in actual practice, it was the Spanish crown that decided who went to the missions and which erring members of the clergy went back to Spain. In other words, the dividing line between spiritual and material authority became thinner and thinner.

For example, a royal representative was always present when the Franciscans elected their religious prelates. If the one elected was not approved of by the royal government, a second election was needed. The temptation, therefore, was to choose someone acceptable to the government even though he was not necessarily qualified, lest they repeat the election. This effectively inhibited true religious discipline.

There was also the story of Archbishop Hernando Guerrero of Manila, a man ready to die to defend church discipline and freedom. The governor general, Sebastián Hurtado de Corcuera, did his job just as resolutely to prevent, as he said, bishops and friars from "interfering" in the government.

Soon the two were at loggerheads over who had the authority to appoint to vacancies in the church. The archbishop claimed he had the right to appoint to a parish, the governor general denied that right. The audiencia was involved. But the archbishop insisted he had the last say. To solve matters, the governor general sent troops to hustle off the prelate and maroon him in exile. That done, he ordered his appointee to take possession of his ecclesiastical office, and sent a report to the king. On 30 May 1640, a royal document arrived in Manila. It warned the archbishop to

conduct yourself with greater circumspection and restraint, extending to all officials . . . the cooperation which is due. . . . And rest assured that if this my admonition does not suffice to restrain and moderate your behavior, I shall be forced to take stronger measures.

No stronger rebuke, a historian wrote, had ever been made to a high church prelate. Mercifully, Archbishop Guerrero had already died. But it showed how jealously the king guarded the regalias and wanted to control everything, including the church.

## The Galleon Trade

Trade in Oriental goods was one reason why the Spaniards colonized the Philippines. But the fact that they were soon engaged in shipping yearly to Mexico, Oriental goods brought by the Chinese to Manila, was not planned.

It started in 1572 when Chinese junks with Oriental goods arrived in Manila a year after Legazpi had founded the city. Reloading the Chinese goods in boats bound for Mexico, the Manila Spaniards earned profits of as much as 300 percent when their goods were sold. Thus was born the galleon trade which lasted until 1815, and a commerce that saved the colony from bankruptcy.

At first, no regulations controlled the trade. But by 1600, laws were issued specifying the amount and kind of goods allowed for sale in Mexico. In 1593, the *permiso,* or permit to trade, limited the value of the cargo to 250,000 pesos, with the *situado* not exceeding 500,000 pesos. The situado was the tax on the goods arriving in Mexico, which was sent back to Manila to help defray government expenses.

This limitation was set because the textile merchants in southern Spain who felt the pinch from the competition of the cheaper Chinese silk brought to Mexico, had lobbied successfully to lower the permiso.

Then in 1606, the situado was set at 500,000 pesos. But part of this revenue also went to funds for *obras pías* or charitable foundations, legacies, and donations. This meant a significant decrease in what the government got from the situado.

In 1640, a royal official uncovered anomalies, and he recommended strict measures to control the traffic. The Manila traders boycotted the royal order and stopped sending goods to Mexico. This forced the government to increase the permiso to 300,000 pesos and the corresponding situado to 600,000 pesos.

The law said one thing; however, people did another. For example, the galleons captured by English buccaneers clearly carried goods valued at as much as 1 million pesos!

One could trade if one had the *boleta* or license issued by a *Junta de repartimiento* (Allotment Board). Spanish widows, orphans, and other Spaniards living on charity also received the boleta. But they did not have the ready cash to buy the goods. Although illegal, they sold their rights to those who had money.

The government eventually closed its eyes to the anomaly. Soon, only a small group of capitalists engaged in the trade. In 1586, there were 194 traders. In 1780, about 200 years later, only 28 monopolists continued investing in the business. They not only controlled the business; worse, they refused to modernize the system lest they lose control of the monopoly.

What were the goods that fetched such high prices in Mexico? Chinese silk, fine cotton from India, exquisitely embroidered Philippine piña, Chinese porcelain, spices, and medicinal herbs comprised the bulk of the cargo.

Profits were so high that the Spaniards remained in Manila to invest in the trade instead of engaging in the more physically taxing agricultural industries in the provinces. That is why, except for the Spanish friars, hardly any peninsular Spaniards resided outside of Manila. And the authority of the church outside the capital explains the pervasive influence of Catholicism on the lives of the ordinary Filipinos.

The galleon trade was for Spaniards only. Although the distance from Spain to the islands discouraged Spanish migrants, the prospect of immediate wealth from the galleon trade nevertheless attracted them to the Philippines. It was not the Filipino, then, who gained wealth from the galleon trade, but the few Spaniards who controlled it.

The colony was poor and failed to raise enough revenue to balance the accounts. For example, in 1584, while public expenses totaled 41,831 pesos, incomed reached only 33,000 pesos. About a hundred years later, in 1637, expenses reached 850,734 pesos, while the government income was only 247,700 pesos. And in 1790, the expenses reached 60,000 pesos, but the revenue was only 411,384 pesos. But the situado helped. Otherwise, the Spaniards would have abandoned the Philippines.

While the situado eased the government's financial problems, the galleon trade made individual traders rich. A Jesuit reported in 1627 that "from the time the Philippines was conquered, it has never been as prosperous and as opulent as it is today." He mentioned silken decor in churches and gold and silver utensils in private houses. Gold stirrups were fashionable, and some families were known to have more than 100 domestic servants.

In the 1660s, there were at least twenty-four cattle ranches near Manila. Some had as many as 4,000 head. The animals were so many that farmers had great difficulty fencing their crops to keep away the freely roaming beasts.

There was, of course, the dark side of the picture. While large fortunes were made on one successful voyage, they could also be ruined in a single disaster. Rich families suddenly became beggars, living in proud destitution and hunger, rather than going to the fields to till the land. Men indulged in gambling, hoping to recoup their losses at sea. Manila swarmed with vagrants. Like their Spanish counterparts, they hoped for a quick strike and stayed around to grab the first chance for a sudden profit. And the temptation for them to engage in underhanded deals was strong, conniving with the Filipino servants who stole from their Spanish masters what they then sold to the first buyer.

The galleon trade meant more than this, however. Wood was needed to build the ships. Where did it come from? From the Philippine forests, which provided the world famous hardwood, the molave. And, even if the boat captain was a Spaniard, chances were that the rest of the crew were native-born Filipinos.

### Rich Traders and Poor Farmers

Because their former tribal followers had been freed from their control when they became vassals of the Spanish crown, the gobernadorcillos or barangay heads lost the men to cultivate the lands the government had granted to them. A few managed to keep their property. But many, no longer with the means to work the land, sold their land.

Spanish landowners, too, decided to rid themselves of their property. They preferred investing in the galleon trade for which they needed ready cash. They, too, sold their lands.

The friars, on the other hand, intended to stay permanently in the Philippines. Because government support for their missions was never enough, they had to look for other sources of revenue. By force, then, of circumstance, and in an age when wealth was in the form of land, the missionary orders in the Philippines had to obtain land, and they became landowners.

Philippine society, therefore, was split between the rich and the poor—the *indios*, as the Spaniards called the native-born Filipinos. The indios had no share in the galleon trade and owned no lands. They lived in the farms, in nipa huts built *bajo la campana* (within hearing of the church bells).

Generally they tilled land for someone else with whom they shared the harvest, or supported themselves as daily wage earners. They engaged in a small-scale economy known as the *tianggi*.

Unlike the daily public market introduced by Spain, the tianggi was held only once a week. People from the uplands offered gold dust, wax, and other forest products. From the coastal areas came those who had fish and other sea products, or salt. And people from the valleys or riverine settlements brought basic foods, fowl, tobacco, earthenware, and some brass work.

Apparently money did not change hands, for one set of goods was bartered for another. Unsold articles in one tianggi were brought to the next tianggi close by. If they traveled by water, the traders loaded their products onto bancas, rafts, or cascos. If by land, men put their produce in baskets swaying at both ends of a pole they shouldered, while women perched large flat winnowing baskets or *bilao* laden with goods, on their heads.

The tianggi was small-scale economy. No matter how strong a person was, his basket-load of products could never earn him a thousand pesos. And people engaged in it, not necessarily for profit, but to obtain basic needs. There were no middlemen, no fixed rates. It was economy by direct exchange.

Meanwhile, the former followers of the datus became tenants, lessees, sharecroppers, or farm laborers. Farm workers could be one of three classes: salaried or nonsalaried workers, *inquilinos,* or *reservas.*

The first two classes were easy to identify. They owned no property, but supported themselves by the sweat of their brow.

The inquilino was one who remained on the land, which might have been his former property but which he had sold to another. He owned a house and, by agreement with the new landowner, he hired the farm hands whom he, not the landowner, paid. If he rented the land for at least nine years, he was called *arrendatario,* usually paying no fees for the first four or five years. His lease included adjacent grazing and wood lands.

The inquilinos were the equivalent of the commercial middlemen. Like the latter, they also became rich. They had workers or *kasama* on their own terms. The harvest belonged to them, although they paid fees to the landowner. By 1790, they were renting extensive areas. Already in 1600, there were several Chinese inquilinos, those descended from a racially mixed marriage and those who married into Filipino families in order to own land. The most famous inquilino in Philippine history is perhaps Don Francisco Mercado of Calamba, Laguna, José Rizal's father.

Then there were the reservas. All able-bodied men, between eighteen and sixty years of age, were obliged to work as polistas for forty, later only, fifteen days. The polistas worked either on government projects, or on friar lands. If on the latter, they were listed as *reservas de polo.*

Polistas worked one day a week, but were paid if they worked more. In the Ilocos and Pampanga, they worked four days a week at one-half real a day. Since the government was not a good paymaster, many preferred being reservas because treatment was better. Then they were allowed to build houses on the land where they worked. By 1608, the reservas' houses had coalesced into civil towns. Of course there was the possibility of collusion, and ghost estates were listed with reserved workers in the official registers.

As the Spaniards planned it, the town had two main sections. The first was the town proper (población, cabecera, or matriz). In it one would find the inquilino and his family who owned the biggest house. Then one would see the nipa and bamboo houses of the reservas and other paid workers close by. During the planting and harvesting weeks, there would be an influx of farm workers from other places. They would come and hire themselves out on a contractual basis, then would leave after the work was over.

These houses, which in time became municipalities, were built around a town plaza, on one side of which was the church, the biggest edifice built for kilometers around. Beside the plaza, too, were the cabildo (townhall) and the public school.

Noticeably absent was the landowner who resided in Manila and who periodically collected either personally or through a representative the fees and a share in the harvest. Not infrequently such a visit called for some kind of celebration among the tenants. It was also the time to readjust or renew the lease.

The second sector of the town would be the fields (sementeras). There one would likely see a large farmhouse (casa de la estancia), often occupied by the inquilino. Close by would be a small storehouse for the farm equipment and miscellaneous tools. There would also be bunks for cowherds (vaqueros), who were paid a monthly salary. In some farms there would be a sugar mill, but all sementeras had a shed (camarín) for storing the harvests. Not a few had an irrigation system complete with canals to bring in water from a dam (presa). Finally, there would be an horno or oven to bake tiles and bricks. This was operated by a team of four workers paid monthly. The master operator received 2 pesos, 6 reales, while the assistants only 1 peso, or 1 peso and 4 reales. They also received food rations and were provided with a carabao for hauling wood and mud.

In 1700, Tondo province (including present-day Rizal, Kalookan, San Mateo, Antipolo, eastern Taguig, the shore area of the Lake of Ba'i, Muntinlupa, and Las Piñas) measured 103,600 hectares. It had a population of 31,000 in twenty-nine towns, the biggest of which was Pasig. In Tondo, 66,045 hectares were owned by 8,000 families who used the land as rice and grazing land. If all of these families farmed, each family would own only 7.25 hectares. If only 6,000 families farmed, each would own a little more—9.5 hectares. But some had more, others less than the average of either 7.25 or 9.5 hectares. Clearly the farmers in old Tondo province were poor. They were representative of a group which was distinct from the small class of wealthy monopolists of the galleon trade and which formed the majority of the Philippine population.

### Suggestions for Further Reading

*(Complete information on recommended readings appears in the bibliography at the end of the book.)*

Arcilla, José S., "Christian missions to China and the Philippines," *PS* 31; Bauzon, Leslie E., *Deficit government: Mexico and the Philippines situado, 1606–1804;* Bernad, Miguel A., *The Christianization of the Philippines;* De la Costa, Horacio V., "The legal basis of Spanish imperial sovereignty," *PS* 1; De la Costa, Horacio V., "Patronato real and recurso de fuerza," in *Asia and the Philippines;* McCoy, Alfred W., and Ed C. de Jesus (eds.), *Philippine social history: Global trade and local transformations;* Quiason, Serafin D., "The tiangui: A preliminary view of an indigenous rural marketing system in the Spanish Philippines," *PS* 33; Quiason, Serafin D., *English "country trade" with the Philippines, 1644–1765;* Schurz, William L., *The Manila galleon.*

# 7
## HISPANIZATION

### The New Habitat

Instead of a unified Philippine nation, the Spaniards found separate, mutually hostile and independent tribes with their own indigenous culture. But the Spaniards did not think these people were "civilized" (from the Latin *civilis*, a word referring to one who lived in the city, *civitas*) simply because the people did not live in cities.

Instead of cities, people lived on coastal strips or along the rivers. To Christianize or govern them better, the Spaniards relocated the people in towns and made them build houses around a central plaza.

At first, these were simple nipa and bamboo structures, even in Manila. But after fire had destroyed the city in 1583, stone or brick edifices began to appear. However, even until the end of the Spanish government, the poor in the provinces, with very few exceptions, continued to live in nipa and bamboo huts.

In general, the Filipinos could be classified into two groups: those who lived in the town (población or cabecera); and those in the barrios which were more or less distant, more or less isolated, and therefore were infrequently in contact with the church or civil authorities.

The rural population were either tenants or small independent farmers. Some who lived by the river or on the seashore earned a meager living by fishing.

Their houses were simple bamboo and nipa structures held up by four harigues or posts, with walls and a roof of cogon or nipa. Bamboo fences marked, their small lot from that of their neighbor's. Sometimes they had a well or a ditch from which they obtained water.

An ordinary house would have only one room, its floor of split bamboo slats tied side by side. A clay stove was in a corner or, if they had one, on the *batalan* or raised narrow back porch. One would also find pestles and a wooden mortar for threshing rice, a small grindstone for corn, a bilao (winnowing basket), a rattan hammock, perhaps a rattan stool, and a wooden bench alongside the *dingding* or wall. Meals would be taken on a table about twelve or eighteen inches high. Light at night came from a small wicker in a clay or brass lamp fed by coconut oil or beeswax. A long bamboo cane was kept filled with water; several bottles might also be in the house for holding tuba (nipa wine). A few plates or pots would also be available; perhaps there would be no forks or spoons. There would, however, be one or two bolos. There would be no beds, but in one corner of the house, one would find one or two *petates* or mats, rolled around pillows and folded blankets and mosquito nets. Finally, there would be a simple family altar, with its sacred images or pictures, one or two devotional books in the native language or Spanish.

In contrast, towards the later centuries of Spanish rule, the houses of rich Filipinos could perhaps be best exemplified by the fictional Capitán Tiago's house, which Rizal described in his novel, *Noli me tangere*:

> The house was large enough, in a style common to those parts . . . rather squat. . . . A wide staircase, green-banistered and partly carpeted, rose from the tiled court at the entrance. It led to the main floor along a double line of potted plants and flower vases set on stands of Chinese porcelain . . . . At the head of the stairs the visitor would have found himself in a spacious entrance hall . . . paintings crowded on the walls, depicting such religious themes as *Purgatory, Hell, The Last Judgment.* . . . The main reception room had great mirrors and sparkling chandeliers. On a pinewood platform stood enthroned a magnificent grand piano, for which an enormous sum had been paid. . . . Furniture was elegant.

Towns usually had three important buildings: the church with an adjoining parish house, the tribunal (town hall), and the school. Prehispanic society did not have places reserved for worship, and in the beginning Philippine churches were usually simply mission structures of nipa and bamboo. In time, more solid churches of brick and mortar were built. The priest's residence was close by, oftentimes adjacent to the church. Since most parish priests were members of the religious orders, the Philippine rectory became popularly known as the *convento*. A bell tower was built either contiguous to the church or as a separate structure. As a precaution against earthquakes and typhoons, churches were built in the "earthquake baroque" style—thick but low walls, round, heavy pillars, and small windows. It was cool inside, and whenever the Moros raided a seacoast town, it served as the people's hiding place.

The second important building in the town was the tribunal. In many towns, they were of bamboo or wood and nipa, but in several provincial capitals they were of solid materials. The tribunal served as: (a) a hall for the sessions of the local government or the court trials; (b) the local jail; and (c) the lodging place for travelers or higher government officials visiting the town. If the tribunal was a fragile structure of bamboo and nipa, a prisoner could easily escape to freedom.

By law, each town had to build two schools, one for boys and another for girls, to teach them Spanish and the Christian catechism. But there were never enough trained teachers; and several provincial schools were mere sheds open to the rain, without walls, floors, or benches. Naturally, this discouraged attendance at school, and until the end of Spanish rule, illiteracy was high in the provinces where few learned Spanish.

With one or two exceptions, houses in the towns were almost always of light inflammable materials, built close to one another, with not enough intervening space to stop flames from spreading. Ordinances and warnings were repeatedly issued, but they remained unheeded. And in spite of the official policy to relocate the people in towns, or at least *bajo campana* (near enough to be able to hear the church bells), most Filipinos lived in their distant farms in mountains or forests. Naturally, they failed to receive the regular teaching of Christian doctrine and the sacraments in the town church on Sundays and feast days, while their children did not attend school. This explains in part why, although loyal to the Christian faith, many Filipinos did not understand it enough, and superstitions or even pagan practices survived.

## The Missions Become Towns

Philippine towns, then, consisted of a central sector (the población) and several outlying barrios. It was, of course, more difficult to govern or to provide the proper religious instruction to those living in the farther barrios. More barrios naturally meant more tributes, but it also meant more difficulty in collecting them. And with population growth, missionaries found it harder to visit all the barrios. Not surprisingly, criminals tended to hide in the more distant barrios. For better government, then, areas that totaled at least 500 tributes (or, after 1844, 1,000 *cédulas personales*) were organized into a separate municipality, distinct from the matrix.

To qualify for the rank of an independent civil town, a barrio or group of barrios had to have a church with a priest's residence, a townhall, a boys' school, and a girls' school. Streets had to be straight and at right angles to one another, and in such a way that they could be extended as the number of houses increased. The town had to be near a good water source and land for farming and grazing.

The process towards township started when the barrio leaders submitted to the provincial governor or alcalde mayor a signed petition, with proof that the proposed town had the minimum requirements. The parish priest's favorable opinion or *visto bueno* was immediately sought; if it was given, the provincial chief countersigned the petition and forwarded it to Manila. The governor general then asked the director of civil administration for his opinion. If everything was in order, the governor general gave his provisional approval and sent the documents or *expediente* to Madrid for royal confirmation. Elections were then held for the local officials.

Not all petitions were approved. Often, despite claims of the petitioners, there was no church, or townhall, or school. (In defense, the petitioners would say they had not yet erected the public buildings for lack of time). Moreover, the men were often absent from the barrio, occupied by the polo in the población. Not only that; the polo was not always carried out for the public good, but to satisfy an abusive gobernadorcillo's personal whims. In such a case, barrio leaders thought of township as a way of severing their barrio's ties with the old town because they could no longer endure the abuses of the town officials.

Sometimes, the gobernadorcillo opposed the petition because it meant fewer tributes in his area of responsibility. Opposition was voiced also because in a new town, it was easy for the barrio leaders to rig the town elections. The usual trick was for the candidates to agree among themselves that candidate A would be elected one year, candidate B the next, candidate C the third, and so on. In this way, together they monopolized public offices.

The creation of new civil towns did not automatically mean the erection of independent parishes. There were never enough priests in the country, and for years, many towns did not have resident pastors. This was true, for example, of the town of Zaragoza (today of the province of Nueva Ecija) which had been the barrio of San Vicente. They asked to be an independent town because they were Ilocanos and could not get along with the others in Aliaga, Nueva Ecija. In 1880, San Vicente separated from Aliaga and became the town of Zaragoza, but it was only after several years that it had a resident priest.

Sometimes, it was the other way around. A new parish with its own resident priest would be erected ahead of the creation of a new civil town. After a few years, the local leaders would petition them that their parish be made a new municipality.

Many of our towns today were founded in the 1860s. Generally, human intrigue and ambition were important factors in the creation of new towns. Barrio leaders did not always live in harmony with their town leaders. Sometimes, barrios wanted to secede because of an abusive gobernadorcillo. Or barrio leaders wanted to be in control in order, like their higher officials, to manipulate the polo. Moreover, they also wanted to control the local elections. Furthermore, although barrio heads received commissions for collecting tributes (and later, the cedulas) for submission to the gobernadorcillo, this only whetted their appetites for a larger share. One can see, therefore, that the growth of the missions into towns was spurred by many factors, not the least of which was the drive for personal gain!

## Schools and Other Social Indicators

Schools are a good index of a country's progress. Jean Baptiste Mallat, the French traveler, was surprised at how advanced Philippine schools were in 1846. But since it was the missionaries who opened the first schools in our country, naturally, they emphasized teachings of the Christian catechism. However, they also taught the people how to read and write in Spanish or in their own languages using the Roman alphabet.

The Augustinians opened a school immediately upon arriving in Cebu in 1565. The Franciscans arrived in 1577, and they, too, immediately taught the people how to read and write, besides imparting to them important industrial and agricultural techniques. The Jesuits who arrived in 1581 also concentrated on teaching the young, for whom they opened the first boarding schools for native children in Panay and Leyte and in Antipolo, outside Manila. And when the Dominicans arrived in 1587, they did the same thing in their first mission in Bataan.

Between 1600 and 1865, there was little change in the Philippine educational system. There were colleges in Manila, like Santa Potenciana for girls or, for boys, Colegio de San José and Universidad de San Ignacio run by the Jesuits, as well as Colegio de San Juan de Letrán and Universidad de Santo Tomás run by the Dominicans. Through the years, these universities and colleges graduated many important colonial officials and church prelates, bishops and archbishops, several of whom served the church in South America.

The rest of the archipelago had no system of public schools simply because the colony could not yet afford it. For more than two centuries, then, Philippine schools were hardly more than catechetical centers. But this was true all over the world, for there were no elementary schools as we understand the term today.

In 1865, the government inaugurated the Escuela Normal (Normal School), an institute to train future primary school teachers. At the same time, primary schooling was made obligatory for all children. In 1867, a royal decree appointed the parish priests as inspectors of local schools. As with other reform laws, the decree failed. There were never enough school funds, teachers' salaries were low, many Normal School graduates preferred working in business corporations for higher wages, parents showed little interest in their children's schooling, and there were never enough classrooms, desks, blackboards, books, etc.

In 1865, the Escuela Municipal, the primary school run by the Jesuits for the city of Manila, was raised to the rank of a secondary school and renamed Ateneo Municipal, with power to grant the arts degree, equivalent to today's Associate of Arts degree in the American system.

The Ateneo, though financed by government funds, was a "private" secondary school, for there was only one "public" secondary school, the University of Santo Tomás. Private secondary schools were classified as "first class" if they offered all the subjects needed to obtain the bachelor's degree, like the Ateneo. A school that offered only a few of these subjects was classified as "second class."

Manila boasted of two institutions of higher learning offering professional studies in law, medicine, or the priesthood: the Jesuit Universidad de San Ignacio and the Dominican Universidad de Santo Tomás. But when the Jesuits were expelled from the Philippines in 1768, the Archbishop of Manila took over the Jesuit colleges, so that only Santo Tomás has enjoyed an unbroken existence since 1611.

Aside from what we may gather about Philippine society in the 1800s from the educational system at the time, what other indicators could help us derive a good picture of Philippine life then?

Politically, in 1812, the Philippines became a Spanish province, and all Filipinos (at the time, a term which referred to pure-blooded Spaniards in the Philippines) were legal citizens or Spaniards, with the right of representation in the Spanish legislative body, the Cortes.

In the area of transportation, in 1834, Manila, Iloilo, Cebu, and Legazpi were officially opened to foreign shipping. Governor Pascual Enrile (1830–48) initiated a road-building program. And in 1848, steamboats arrived, finally putting an end to the vinta raids from Mindanao and Sulu.

In communications, a weekly mail service was started in 1833. Every Monday, at noon, mounted carriers left Manila for the northern Luzon provinces; every Wednesday noon, another group of carriers rode to the southern Luzon provinces. The return mail from the north arrived on Friday, while that from the south on Tuesday. Mail to the Visayas, the Batanes, and the Marianas Islands was sent on the first boat available. Daily mail was possible only from Manila to Cavite and vice versa.

Public utilities improved in 1882, when Francisco Carriedo y Peredo installed a water system in Manila. Telephone service began in 1890, electricity in 1895. In 1873, a direct steamship line through the Suez Canal was inaugurated between Spain and the Philippines, while the Manila-Dagupan railway, started in 1887, was finished in 1892.

The first Philippine newspaper was *Del Superior Gobierno*, but it lasted for only fifteen issues. The first daily newspaper was *La Esperanza* (1846), followed by *La Estrella* (1847), and *Diario de Manila* (1848), the last one 42.5 cm by 26.5 cm in size. The first bilingual paper in Tagalog and Spanish, *Diariong Tagalog*, published by Marcelo H. del Pilar and Basilio Teodoro, appeared in June 1882. But it folded up the following October for lack of subscribers, due probably to a severe typhoon and an equally severe epidemic.

And what of fashion in those days? Foreigners marveled at the beauty of the native Filipina with her "luxuriant black hair and large dark eyes." Ordinary women's clothes were the *tapis*, drawn closely around the body, paired with a bodice of embroidered native cloth; embroidered slippers adorned the feet. Ordinary female ornaments were religious medals and scapulars.

Filipino male attire ordinarily consisted of a hat, trousers, and a shirt of coarse guimara cloth. Richer Filipinos wore the more expensive jusi or piña shirt. They had a *salakot*, a large stiff hat neatly woven out of reeds serving as an umbrella or sunshade, depending on the weather. Those who could afford to, decorated it with silver.

The principalia wore an official black jacket over the shirt, plus a tall cylindrical hat, yellowed with age, an heirloom of the family and sign of their honored status in the town. Leather shoes from Europe were not unknown. Younger men wore tight-fitting trousers with black or bright-colored stripes, a stiff starched shirt imported from Europe, and a stovepipe silk hat. A walking stick completed the ensemble.

Filipinos in general were musically inclined. Many could sing; many played one, even five musical instruments. In every town there was a small group of musicians who formed themselves into a band. They played during the Mass and at fiestas and processions. Sometimes, if a church had no organ, the town band or *rondalla* played music not always proper for the religious ceremonies or helpful to prayer, like the lighthearted pieces from the French comic operas.

Besides vocal and instrumental music, the Filipinos were gifted dancers. They had several dances. The *kumintang* was a love dance; the *pampango* was accompanied by the clapping of hands; and the Visayan *bagay* was accompanied by the loud and wild cries of the dancers themselves.

What we call minority groups today who continued to live in the mountains had their own musical traditions. Most important were the rites before planting, when they invoked the gods for propitious weather. Likewise, they held war dances just before raiding a hostile tribe close by.

Indeed, although Hispanization might have changed indigenous customs to some extent, it had not totally eradicated them. But local idioms clearly show Hispanic influences, and many external manifestations of the Catholic faith are also clearly Hispanic.

## Suggestions for Further Reading

*(Complete information on recommended readings appears in the bibliography at the end of the book.)*

Fenner, Bruce L., *Cebu under the Spanish flag: 1521–1896*; Filipiniana Book Guild, *Travel accounts of the islands, 1513–1787*; Gemelli Carreri, Giovanni Franceso, *A voyage to the Philippines*; Jagor, Fedor, *Travels in the Philippines*; La Gironiere, Paul P. de, *Twenty years in the Philippines*; Le Gentil, Guillaume, *A voyage to the Indian seas*; Marche, Alfred, *Luzon and Palawan*; Phelan, John L., *The Hispanization of the Philippines: Spanish aims and Filipino responses, 1565–1700*; Wernstedt, Frederic L., and J. E. Spencer, *The Philippine island world: A physical, cultural, and regional geography*.

# 8

## ECONOMIC GROWTH

### Early Economic Development

Like the Dutch, the British formed an East India Company, one purpose of which was to engage in the profitable China trade. But to stanch the outflow of English silver, they bartered English iron goods or Indian cotton textiles for Asian pearls or spices, which the Chinese accepted in exchange for tea. But this meant the British had to have an eastern port or base of operation not yet occupied by either the Spaniards or the Dutch.

Then war broke out between England and Spain. This fitted into British commercial plans. They decided to supply men and arms to the East India Company, and to send an expedition under the command of Rear Admiral Samuel Cornish to conquer Manila. Once taken, Manila would be handed over to Dawsonne Drake, a civilian official of the trading company.

On 22 September 1762, a squadron of eight warships, three frigates and two supply ships, with a landing force of about 1,000 British regulars, 300 marines, 600 Sepoys, and 40 volunteers of other nationalities, appeared in Manila bay. No news of any hostilities had been received, and Manila was completely taken unawares. Except for 556 Mexicans and 85 Filipino gunners, there was no defense. Four companies of 75 men each and native auxiliaries from the provinces were hastily recruited.

The Spanish forces were no match for the unerring British artillery. Archbishop Manuel Antonio Rojo, who was acting as the governor general, was forced to surrender. He was told to pay a ransom of 4 million pesos. But before surrendering, he commissioned Simón Anda y Salazar, one of the *oidores* of the audiencia, to keep the provinces loyal to Spain. The latter slipped through the lines and organized a resistance movement based in Bulacan and Pampanga. He also managed to warn the galleon *Filipina* returning with silver from Acapulco, thus preventing it from falling into enemy hands.

The British occupation of Manila did not last long. The European war ended just a few months after the British had taken Manila. On 12 June 1764, the British had departed from the city.

But the British invasion had ruined the Philippine economy. No galleon arrived or left during the two years of British occupation. To add to the distress, the two galleons had been captured by the British: *Covadonga*, with more than 1.35 million pesos, and *Santísima Trinidad*, with cargo valued at more than 3 million pesos. Farmlands had been burned or left untilled, livestock had been killed, and the merchant community was penniless. Famine threatened the land, while bandits roamed the countryside.

Luckily, Charles III of Spain was an able king and his governors were resourceful men. Convinced the Philippines could not continue to depend on the galleon trade, they initiated what we today would call "socioeconomic development programs."

In 1769, the king approved the Consulado (Chamber of Commerce) of Manila, a different entity from the traditional "City and Commerce of Manila," which from the beginning had cared for the commercial interests of the colony. Membership in the new body was open only to married *criollos* (or those born in the country of Spanish parents) and the Gachupines (Latin Americans with at least ten years' residence in the Philippines). Unfortunately, although never more than fifty, they succeeded in blocking efforts to modernize the economy.

In 1770, Simón de Anda came back as governor of the colony. He encouraged private enterprise, subsidizing individual entrepreneurs like Francisco Javier Salgado, who manufactured plowshares and cannonballs from the iron mined at Angat, Bataan, or the Augustinian Fray Matías Octavo, the first to produce indigo in quantity.

Governor José Basco y Vargas succeeded Anda as governor in 1778. He organized the Sociedad Económica de Amigos del País (Patriotic Economic Society). It provided funds to improve agriculture, offered prizes for the most abundant sugar or coffee harvests, and even conducted model farms. Influenced by the contemporary European fad to promote "profitable" education (we would say, "vocational" or "technical" training), the society financed schools for painting and music.

But the most successful project was the tobacco monopoly introduced in 1782. Basco ordered that only tobacco should be grown in Cagayan and Nueva Ecija. Since the government could not completely stop tobacco farms in Mindanao and the Visayas, tobacco raisers were obliged to sell their produce to the government.

Government agents graded the leaf, paid for it at government prices, destroyed what was not needed, and stored the good ones in government warehouses. The leaf was rolled into cigars and cigarettes in government factories, and the finished product was sold or exported in government shops or *estanquillos*.

It was so successful that in 1783, a year after the project started, the government had a surplus of 1,310,656 pesos after overdue accounts had been paid. Seven years later, the sum of 1,297,772 pesos was sent to Spain. For the first time, the Philippines ceased being an economic drag on the royal treasury and was, instead, a source of substantial income, in cash, credit, or in the form of cigars and tobacco leaf that sold easily.

But abuses soon were rife. Tobacco growers were usually unpaid, or paid at very low rates. Smuggling and contraband sales could not be contained. An entire army of government functionaries had to be mobilized to supervise the entire operation: revenue agents, tobacco graders, factory supervisors, transport inspectors, etc. These needed a salary which raised government expenses.

But it did turn the economy around. It also occasioned the start of an internal trade. Regions where the best land was reserved for tobacco became markets for products grown elsewhere, like rice, which soon began to be needed in commercial quantities.

## Sugar and Abaca

In 1776, the boat *Buen Consejo* successfully sailed around Africa and reached Manila in half the time previously needed for the Manila-Acapulco-Sevilla trajectory. This brought royal supervision closer to the Philippines, and people did not like it.

But Madrid was determined to improve the colonial economy. In 1785, the Royal Philippine Company was inaugurated. Its boats were allowed to sail directly to China, putting an end to the old practice of waiting in Manila for the Chinese junks to bring in the goods for reshipment to Acapulco. Trade, therefore, was liberalized and old monopolies were threatened. For lack of interest, however, the company was dissolved some years later. Besides, the French Revolution had already started.

Foreign boats docked frequently in Manila by 1790. Soon, foreign merchants left agents behind, who contracted with native sugar growers for when the boats returned. At first, the foreign agents worked either by themselves or with help from native, Chinese, or even Spanish contractors. Later, the agents advanced capital to enable native planters to increase production.

Thus we see a development in the sugar industry. First, it was simply buy-and-sell. Then, a middleman made the arrangements. Finally, capital was loaned. What else was this but modern trade methods?

During the Napoleonic Wars (1789–1815), trade with Europe diminished. This allowed home industries to grow. In 1819, Bulacan had an estimated 500 looms in operation, employing 1,500 women spinners and 2,000 weavers, and producing cotton, silk, and piña cloth. Baliwag was a center for *buri* hats.

The Spanish Colonel Ildefonso de Aragón described Philippine domestic trade from 1819 to 1821 this way:

> There is hardly a town in the province of Pangasinan from which itinerant merchants do not set out yearly for Lingayen. To it they bring the gold of the Agno River and the Igorot mines, many pack loads of deer meat or *tapa*, and great quantities of deer skins. On reaching a town they dismount at the *tribunal*, divide their merchandise among themselves, and each one shoulders his pack to go from house to house. They spare no pains to make as profitable a sale as they can, and accept payment either in money or in goods, which they hope to sell in Manila. These may be the skins and tapa of Pampanga, the cocoa of Cagayan, the striped cloth and *terlinga* of Ilocos . . . everything on which they reckon they can make money.

Another description by Sinibaldo de Mas, an official in Manila at about the same period, reads,

> Salt, sugar, oil and dried fish are supplied by Pangasinan to the inhabitants of Ilocos, the Cagayan missions, Nueva Ecija and upper Pampanga. The latter exports large quantities of dried deermeat, called *tapa*. Ilocos cotton goes to almost all provinces. The buffaloes of Laguna come for the most part from Nueva Ecija. The indigo of Bulacan and Laguna find an opening in Iloilo, Camarines, and other places. The *piña* and *sinamay* of the last mentioned provinces are luxury articles everywhere. The sailcloth woven in Ilocos and the *abaca* cordage of Albay are likewise in demand for ships' rigging. Certain regions supply others with timber and bamboo.

But the most important development was that of the sugar industry. On 13 July 1856, Nicholas Loney, first British consul in Iloilo, arrived with cheap English cottons to barter for sugar. Moreover, he brought funds and machinery to refine the cane. This naturally mechanized the milling processes and modernized the sugar export industry.

Whether intended or not, Loney's textiles killed the native textile industry in Iloilo, while promoting the sugar industry in Negros. Iloilo soon lost its economic importance, serving only as the port of exchange between the local sugar exporters and the foreign merchants.

Before Loney, Negros produced only 3,000 piculs of sugar every year. In 1880, the island exported 618,120 piculs; and in 1893, 1,800,000. Likewise, in 1850, Negros had only 7 sugar mills; but in 1880, the island had 571; in 1893, 821. This economic activity occasioned a parallel growth in population. In 1850, the population was estimated at about 30,000. In 1880, it jumped to 200,000; and in 1893 to 320,000.

A similar development in abaca production took place in the Bicol provinces. Abaca was first exported in significant quantity in 1818, when it was found to be better for the binder twine needed by the mechanical harvester invented by Richard McCormick. Abaca fiber, thus, became a prime commodity in international trade.

The abaca industry followed a development similar to that of Negros sugar. Foreign importers on both sides of the Atlantic, through their American and British representatives in Manila—for example, Ker and Co.; Peele, Hubble and Co.; Smith, Bell and Co.—made known their orders to paid provincial subagents, who more or less monopolized the product for them. Thus the foreign buyer was able to control the price at the source, while raising its export value.

The abaca industry, however, depended on the world market. If prices went up, for example, between 1865 and 1873, producers and exporters reaped huge profits. But when prices fell, as during the American Civil War of 1861–1865 or the European and American economic depressions in 1857, 1873, and 1893, the industry suffered. Some commercial houses in Manila collapsed. Others with sufficient capital managed to survive and diversified their trade.

Nevertheless, there was a pronounced economic improvement in the entire colony. In 1809, the colonial revenue totaled 2.6 million pesos, while expenses reached 2.8 million pesos. Fifty years later, the revenue was 10 million pesos, but with expenses grown to 10.5 million pesos, the government had incurred a slight deficit. In 1894, two years before the Bonifacio uprising, public revenue reached 13.6 million pesos, and the expenses totaled 13.3 million pesos.

### An Embryonic Middle Class

In 1590, after twenty years as a Spanish colony, the Philippines had an estimated Christian native population of 667,000, distributed among twelve alcaldías: Manila, Balayan (or Batangas), Cagayan, Calilayan (or Tayabas, later Quezon), Camarines, Cebu, Ilocos, Laguna, Masbate, Pampanga, Panay, and Pangasinan. In 1800, the population had grown to 1,561,251. In 1845, the count was 3,488,258. But in 1876, just twenty years after, a more accurate count put the population at 6,173,632, with only about 602,853, or only one out of ten Filipinos not yet Christianized.

While the numerical growth of the Philippine population was comparable to many countries of the world, its culture and economy lagged.

The few Spaniards in the colony had concentrated on the galleon trade. Domestic trade was controlled by the Chinese and Chinese mestizos, and foreign trade was capitalized by foreign houses.

In 1570, there were only about 40 Chinese in Manila. In 1830, they totaled 5,442, and that year sent 136,050 pesos of their earnings to mainland China. If one remembers that the Chinese had been in the Philippines for centuries, one can imagine the great amount of money sent away and lost by the Spanish colonial government of Manila through the years.

The Chinese were some of the first to take advantage of the tobacco, sugar, and abaca export industries. In 1849, 92 percent of the Chinese in the Philippines stayed in Manila. After this date, they spread all over the archipelago. By 1891, 48 percent were in Manila and 12 to 14 percent in the abaca region. Some 1,600 Chinese in the tobacco provinces of Cagayan and Isabela, 476 merchants were based in Misamis, 155 in Cotabato, and 254 in Surigao.

The Chinese acted as middlemen. They took on credit entire stocks of finished foreign goods and retailed them all over the islands. In exchange, they procured the exports from the local producers. Sometimes, they took loans from individual Spanish and foreign capitalists. Before the loan matured, they repaid part of the debt, and took a bigger loan, which they also partly paid soon after, in order to be able to take a third even bigger loan. In this way, over a period of years, their credit was good, since they always paid the loan whether partially or in full.

This was how Chinese and foreign entrepreneurs penetrated the Filipino business sector. For example, soon in Iloilo only six landowners claimed more than 1,000 hectares of sugar land each. In Pampanga, available records show that Chinese mestizos were generally the huge landowners. Similarly in Bicol, foreigners, not Bicolanos, invested in abaca.

In the new economic situation, those who earned more and claimed huge landed properties became important socially. The old principalia, or incumbent and past gobernadorcillos and cabezas de barangay, and their oldest sons who succeeded to their positions, were no longer the élite. Government reforms limited their role to two hateful tasks: the collection of the tribute and the recruitment of polistas. Their judicial powers were vested in municipal courts presided over by new justices of the peace. And financial matters were placed in the hands of a new directory of local administration.

In other words, the gobernadorcillo or cabeza de barangay no longer enjoyed a position of respect or power. Worse, already without economic clout, they continued to represent a government that was becoming more burdensome and hateful. The rich exporters enjoyed no political power, but they had wealth and sent their sons to schools either in Manila or abroad. They studied law, medicine, pharmacy, theology, and became as Spanish as the Spaniards themselves. They spoke, read, wrote Spanish, and were familiar with Hispanic styles and tastes. Their ideal society was a hispanized Philippines, different from that of the poorer, ordinary indio. The new elite, the *ilustrados*, the enlightened and educated group, wanted a Philippines that was, unlike the other Asian countries, strongly Hispanized.

But the Spaniards, criollos or peninsulares, looked down on them. Many of the Filipino elite were at least equally, if not better, educated than their peninsular counterparts, but they were not accepted as equals.

The government hesitated. It could not avoid introducing reforms; it could not continue to govern the colony in the old way. For example, it finally changed the tribute with the *cédula personal*, putting the Filipinos on an equal legal standing as "citizens" of Spain. But law was one thing, implementation another. This discrepancy eventually led to the Philippine Revolution.

## Suggestions for Further Reading

*(Complete information on recommended readings appears in the bibliography at the end of the book.)*

Comyn, Tomás de, *State of the Philippines in 1810;* De Jesus, Edilberto, Jr., *Tobacco monopoly in the Philippines: Bureaucratic enterprise and social change, 1766–1880;* Díaz-Trechuelo, María Lourdes, "The economic development of the Philippines in the second half of the eighteenth century," *PS* 11–14; Owen, Norman G., *Prosperity without progress: Manila hemp and material life in the colonial Philippines.*

# 9

## ROOTS OF A NATION

### Institutions of Hispanization

To carry out its colonial policies, Spain promoted informal and formal education. Informal education was imparted through sermons during Mass and other forms of preaching or teaching in the towns and missions that the missionaries established. Formal education was done through schools and colleges, where at first only the priests taught. Later, lay teachers also were hired.

As mentioned, the problem of languages was solved when the missionaries themselves composed the first Philippine grammars and dictionaries. One of the earliest of these was the *Introducción a la lengua bisaya* written by Fr. Cristóbal Jiménez, one of the first Jesuit missionaries who went to Leyte in 1596. The Dominican, Fr. Juan de la Cruz, who died in 1605, wrote an *Esbozo de un arte en lengua tagalog*.

At first the catechism was taught orally, but books were soon needed. The Dominican Fray Blancas de San José introduced printing to the Philippines, and in 1593, the Dominicans issued the first books ever printed in the country: the *Doctrina cristiana*, in Spanish and Tagalog, and a Chinese edition of the same work. A third work was also printed that year, the *The Real Traditional Propagation of the True Religion* by Fr. Juan Cobo, one of the first missionaries who tried to Christianize the Chinese in the Philippines.

At least 245 different books were published between 1593 and 1750, a total of 157 years. The greatest number were devotional books, like *Reminders of Christian Life*, or *Tagalog Prayers for Communion and Confession*. There were also books of history, mainly of the Christian missions, for example, Fr. Pedro Murillo Velarde's history of the Philippine Jesuit missions (1749), or Fray Pedro Aduarte's history of the Dominican missionary work (1640). There were books on lives of saints and martyrs, especially those recently martyred in China in 1747–1748; there were catechetical books, grammars, dictionaries, including a Japanese dictionary; there were books on the laws of the church, published because of the chronic fights between the state and the church in the

Philippines; and there was one curious book about diseases in the missions, with suggestions on their cure, using only indigenous medicinal herbs and plants.

By 1750, about two centuries after the Spaniards had introduced Christianity and Spanish law, natives like Tomás Pinpin of Bataan and a few other Tagalog writers were writing or publishing books. All the other authors were Spanish, mostly missionaries and a few government officials. Pinpin began as Fr. Blancas de San José's assistant, but soon learned to manage the printing press. He wrote the *Book on How Tagalogs May Learn the Spanish Language* in 1610.

Authors who were friars or priests would naturally write mainly devotional books to spread Christianity or to strengthen the people's faith. If we keep in mind that practically no Spaniards stayed in the rural towns besides the missionary, it is not surprising that Philippine society became deeply religious.

Life revolved around the yearly fiesta, occurring regularly, often during the harvest season. This was also the time for friends and relatives to come together and celebrate their patron saint's day.

Some of the recreational habits of the Filipinos included gambling, both according to Chinese and Spanish systems. Cockfights were popular, and by Rizal's time, license to operate a cockpit was a yearly monopoly: the concessionaire paid the government a definite sum which he expected to recover from the revenue of the cockfights. The sale of playing cards and the license to hold card games in one's residence were similarly profitable monopolies granted to the highest bidder. And in the beginning, to impress on the people the importance of the sacraments of baptism and matrimony and of Christian burial, the missionaries made them occasions for external celebrations and joyful banquets. In time, the church had to issue laws limiting both the number of these feasts and the manner of holding them, lest they become occasions for debauchery.

The Hispanization of Filipinos only partially succeeded. Not everything that the Spaniards introduced was accepted, and what was adopted was made to suit the local situation. On the other hand, several indigenous customs were respected by the Spaniards, as long as they did not go against the law or Christianity. The best example is the preservation of the prehispanic tribal order, headed by the datu who became the gobernadorcillo or cabeza de barangay. They soon formed the local élite, or the principalia, with specific privileges, like using the honorific title of "Don."

Hispanic Philippines, therefore, was *hierarchical*. Social ranking was taken as a matter of course. Nevertheless, the Spanish style of colonial administrator had its democratic elements.

For example, on 5 December 1740, tribute was fixed at 10 *reales castellanos,* or the equivalent in goods. In some cases, it was merely what the people could afford. The goods acceptable as tribute were: *mantas de abacá* (abaca cloth called *medriñaque)* about 20 feet long, 5 feet wide, equivalent to 3 reales; abaca fiber useful to strengthen cables, six kilos of which were worth 2 reales of tribute money; *lampotes* or cotton cloth about 20 feet long, 3 feet wide, equivalent to 4 reales; and *mantas gruesas de algodón* or thick cotton cloth from Ilocos, useful as sails.

To inform the people of their obligations, the alguacil mayor (chief constable) in the provincial capitals summoned the gobernadorcillos, barangay heads, the principales, and the other important people to a meet with a visitor from Manila. They discussed the law until an agreement was reached. It seems safe to say that the central authorities seldom imposed a new ruling without listening to the views of the people in the towns. If it went against an old custom, Manila was slow or careful not to enforce it.

This happened in Lingayen, Pangasinan in 1744, where at a town meeting, it was agreed to continue the custom of paying 1 real, besides the customary tribute. The extra revenue was set aside for expenses for the annual town elections, the salaries of the government officials, and those who helped in the church. Any amount left was for the celebration of the three big feasts: Holy Thursday, Corpus Christi, and the local patron saint's day. At the same time, the privilege was confirmed for nineteen-year-old males to pay 24 reales or 3 pesos as the fee for exemption from the polo. If still more money remained, it became part of the community fund under the supervision of the parish priest. No one, without proper approval, could use this fund which was reserved for charity and emergency use. But abuses were not rare in the allocation of the fund.

## Stirrings of Nationalism

With the Spanish American colonies finally having won their independence by 1825, the economic link between Acapulco and Manila was severed. But modern ideas continued to flow across the Pacific to Manila. The Philippines could not be shut off forever from liberal movements and revolutions. It was a matter of time before the Filipinos, too, would follow the Latin American example.

In 1821, a manifesto signed by an "Indio agraviado" complained that the indios were not taught Spanish, lest the people could argue on equal terms with the Spaniards. The native people were not permitted to become rich lest they mix with or be on an equal footing with the latter.

The manifesto was soon forgotten, and nothing came out of it. It was, perhaps, too early for *public* complaints or denunciations of government shortcomings.

Two years later, a new governor general arrived in Manila with peninsular (that is, *peninsulares,* those born in the Iberian peninsula) military officers. Mexican officers still loyal to Spain as well as Spaniards born in the Philippines (that is, criollos or *insulares*) were bypassed, and only peninsular Spaniards in the army were promoted. Three disgruntled military officers, Luis Rodríguez de Varela, José Ortega, and Andrés Novales, organized a countermove. Discovered, the first two were immediately repatriated to Spain, while the third was assigned to Mindanao. On 23 June 1823, Novales unexpectedly surfaced, won over a few people to his side, and mutinied. About 800 soldiers joined him, but they were no match for the troops sent against them with reenforcements from the Pampanga regiment. Novales was executed, ending the first open military attempt at government takeover in the Philippines. However, it had been aimed to protect the rights, not of the indios, but rather of the Filipino criollos.

Apolinario de la Cruz was a *donado* or a volunteer aide at the San Juan de Dios hospital. In 1832, he organized a pious confraternity under the patronage of Saint Joseph. Although the group was refused the license to continue as a pious society, its members continued to meet and perform their religious prayers and devotions. The leaders were apprehended, and in 1841, outside the town of Tayabas, a rally was held which the authorities tried to disperse. The members stayed put, willing to die. On 23 October, government troops moved against them. In the riot, the governor of Tayabas (now Quezon) was killed, and de la Cruz, betrayed, was caught, tried, and executed on 4 November. In reviewing the case, however, the higher court in Spain declared it was a religious movement and should have been handled differently.

It was government policy to assign troops to places other than their native provinces. For example, in 1841, it was the Cagayan regiment, not the Tayabas soldiers, who had moved against the Confraternity of Saint Joseph. This led to resentment in the ranks, since several of those killed were relatives of troops serving elsewhere. In 1843, they rose in arms, calling on their officers and their fellow countrymen to fight for "independence." The French consul observed that finally, for the first time, the Filipinos uttered that special word. Again, perhaps it was still too early. For instead of support, the call to mutiny was answered with shots from Filipinos loyal to the government, and the mutineers were forced to surrender.

Thus, for about fifty years before the Cavite Mutiny, the people had not yet united into one political entity, distinct from other nations, and capable of self-rule. The Filipinos were still loyal to Spain and, if they rebelled or took up arms, it was to protest against certain specific ills in the government, not against the government itself.

But preventive arrests alienated many. Several indios, either to save themselves or because they could not stand the situation, migrated to Spain. Among the earliest Filipino residents in Spain were Gregorio Sancianco and the Paterno brothers, Pedro, Alejandro, and Máximo Jr.

The Paterno residence in Madrid was frequented by Spanish literary and political figures. At these reunions Pedro used to read his verses, which he later collected and published in book form titled *Sampaguita*. Their poetic or literary merits are better overlooked for they were not much, but Paterno's book marked the first attempt to express a distinctly *Filipino* personality by one who was Filipino.

More important was the work by Sancianco. He had planned to write a trilogy, but he finished only the first part to which he gave the title *El progreso de Filipinas*. Sancianco analyzed the socioeconomic situation and blamed the outmoded tribute for the underdevelopment of the Philippines. A better financial policy, he indicated, was needed to generate funds for the necessary infrastructure (roads, bridges, etc.) and basic government services (police, schools, better salaries, etc.). With increased government revenue, roads could be built to transport agriculture products to the market, and schools improved.

Sancianco's book was what would be called a feasibility study for a socioeconomic development program. In it he wrote that tax measures were imposed on those who could pay them least, and the tribute, obligatory only for the indios, was a form of racism, outdated and no longer tolerable in modern society.

Just like Paterno's book of verses, Sancianco's was an early expression of Filipinism. His calm, expository style could not hide his deep love for his country. If the Philippines was legally a Spanish province, he noted, its people should be treated as Spanish citizens.

Sancianco's writing, perhaps ahead of its time, failed to impress the government. In fact, he disappeared from history in 1884, probably imprisoned as a result of a local disturbance in Pangasinan. But he enunciated ideas which reappeared in the later nationalist writings of authors like Rizal, whom he clearly influenced.

## The Native Clergy

Even in the early years of Spanish rule in South America, native candidates for the priesthood were immediately ordained. But many of them failed to live up to the demands of the Catholic priesthood; and the bishops, forgetting that they should have offered them better education and training, wrongly concluded that the native priests failed because they were not Europeans but rather indios. Subsequently, because of their race, native candidates were barred from sacred orders.

The Philippines was under the jurisdiction of Mexico, and the same prohibitions were imposed in the country. That was why native candidates were not accepted for priestly ordination. The evangelization, then, of the Philippines was the task almost exclusively of Spanish missionaries.

But conversion of pagans and unbelievers, which was in general the task of missionaries, was just the first step. The converts needed help for them to continue to lead true Christian lives. This was the responsibility of the diocesan or secular priests in charge of parishes, under the direct supervision of the bishop.

When the Philippine church was organized, the bishops became responsible for consolidating the Christian church in the islands. Part of their duty was to visit the parishes. But because there were never enough secular priests, friar missionaries remained in charge of the majority of the Philippine parishes.

This led to the problem of "visitation" and "secularization" of the parishes. Since the missionaries already had their own religious superior, the bishop who came and supervised their work was another superior placed over them. Naturally the missionaries refused to accept a second authority, the bishop. If there had been enough native clergy, the problem would not have arisen. Missions that had grown into stable parishes could be "secularized," or ceded to the diocesan priests, as church law provided. But church law was not followed for lack of native clergy in the Philippines. When the bishop insisted on visiting the parishes, the missionaries threatened to abandon their posts, forcing the bishop to give up visiting the parishes.

Episcopal visitation or secularization of the parishes, unfortunately, became a racial question. Almost all the missionaries were peninsulares, while the parish priests were insulares. Visitation and secularization were thus identified as the "Filipinization" of the parishes.

Then in 1768, the Jesuits were expelled from the Philippines. Priests were needed for about 114 missions and some schools which the Jesuits had been forced to abandon. In spite of good will among the religious orders, there never were enough priests in the Philippines to take the Jesuits' place. Mindanao, for example, was assigned to the Recollects, but they could never muster enough personnel to effectively Christianize the island.

In 1859, the Jesuits returned to the Philippines mainly to resettle and evangelize the unbaptized tribes in Mindanao and the nearby islands. They were to replace the Recollects who, in compensation, would be assigned to parishes elsewhere.

In 1842, seemingly at the government's suggestion, the Recollects, who owned land in Cavite, had asked for parishes there. They said it would help their *definidores* or councillors to stay there since they would be nearer Manila for their regular chapter meetings. The governor general asked the archbishop's opinion, but the latter answered that the Dominicans, too, owned lands in the same province but were not asking for parishes there. The government pounced on this innocent observation, and assigned parishes both to the Recollects and the Dominicans. Unfortunately, these were parishes which for many years had been administered by the secular priests.

In 1862, the parish priest of Antipolo, a secular priest, died. Fr. Pedro Peláez, the vicar general, assigned another secular priest, the criollo Francisco Champmas in his place. But the government refused to confirm him and assigned a Spanish Recollect friar instead. As had happened in 1842, Antipolo, one of the richest parishes and long administered by Philippine-born priests, was transferred to Spanish missionaries.

It was clear the government wanted to completely eliminate or control the native clergy. In 1810, a Philippine-born Mexican priest had instigated the first successful revolution in Latin America against Spain. Fifteen years later, Latin America was completely independent. Only Cuba, Puerto Rico, and the Philippines remained with Spain, which wanted to make sure the same thing did not repeat itself in the Philippines. Native-born Filipino priests were to be slowly eliminated or neutralized.

Despite opposition, however, several native-born Filipinos had already been ordained to the priesthood by the end of the eighteenth century. Of course, some failed to live up to their vocation, but there were several who were good and, in some cases, better than many Spanish priests. Moreover, because they could speak the native tongues, the Filipino priests were closer to the people. They were also suspected of harboring separatist learnings.

Because of the *patronato*, it was cheaper and surer to hold on to the Philippines through Spanish friars than through soldiers. Spanish conservatives, then, joined hands with the liberals to keep the friars in the Philippines. They launched a propaganda campaign against the native clergy, falsely portraying them as inept and even personally immoral, of doubtful political convictions, and of questionable theological views.

Despoiled of their parishes, the Filipino clergy banded to fight the injustice inflicted on them. Their leader was the Laguna-born Fr. Pedro Peláez. He organized the priests to collect funds to send a spokesperson before the Madrid government. He also wrote at least two pamphlets in favor of the Philippine-born priests, besides sending memoranda to the queen. Unfortunately, he died buried under the ruins of the Manila Cathedral which was destroyed by a strong earthquake on 3 June 1863. His place was taken by Fr. José A. Burgos, a young priest born in Ilocos.

## Suggestions for Further Reading

*(Complete information on recommended readings appears in the bibliography at the end of the book.)*

Anderson, Gerald H. (ed.), *Studies in Philippine church history*; Arcilla, José S., "Ateneo de Manila: Problems and policies, 1859–1939," *PS* 32; Arcilla, José S., "The Escuela Pía, forerunner of Ateneo de Manila," *PS* 31; Arcilla, José S., "The exile of a liberal in 1870, or Father Arnedo's case," *PS* 19; De la Costa, Horacio V., and John N. Schumacher, *The Filipino clergy: Historical studies and future perspectives;* Jagor, Fedor, *Travels in the Philippines.;* Repetti, William C., *The beginning of Jesuit education in the Philippines;* Repetti, William C., *The College of San José of Manila;* Robles, Eliodoro G., *The Philippines in the nineteenth century.*

Artist's conception of Magellan's death

The Philippine barangay
*(From a photo taken by Otto Fischer, 1888; procured in Madrid)*

The Central plaza of Vigan, Ilocos Sur

Felipe Segundo Rey de España

Governor Ramon Blanco (1893–96)

Francisco Rizal,
father of the national hero

Rizal's mother in her old age

Native gobernadorcillo

The mestiza

Hand-embroidered image of Theresa of Jesus (ca. 1800),
a sample of the textile industry

Partial view of Cebu

Tuguegarao townhall

Chapel of the arsenal at Cavite

Church of Oton, Iloilo

Tuguegarao primary school

# 10

## THREE NATIONAL HEROES

### José Apolonio Burgos

Fr. José Apolonio Burgos was born in Vigan, Ilocos Sur on 9 February 1837. Not wealthy, his father was a Spanish army lieutenant and his mother, a Spanish mestiza. Orphaned early, the ten-year-old José began schooling at Letrán College in 1847. Five years later, he obtained a scholarship at the University of Santo Tomás, which granted him two doctorates, one in theology and another in canon law in 1871. When Father Peláez died, Father Burgos was appointed rector of the Manila Cathedral, although he had not yet finished his studies. Little is known of his life outside his brief academic career, for he was only thirty-five years old when he was executed in 1872.

In 1864, an anonymous pamphlet was published defending the Filipino clergy against charges that they were inferior or that they were disloyal to Spain. The pamphlet argued that Filipino priests had the legal right to be appointed as parish priests, while friars permanently administering a parish were an anomaly.

It also contended that Filipino priests could be entrusted with the highest tasks in the church. According to the pamphlet, the friars kept denying this in order to perpetuate themselves in the parishes; but no one could deny the record of several good Filipino priests who were

> pure Indios, without any Spanish blood. . . . Masangkay, and a certain Máximo, who were parish priests of this *Sagrario* [the Manila Cathedral], a Torres of the town of Binondo, a Saguinsin of Quiapo, a Rodríguez of Marikina, a Pinpin, an Arámbulo, a Pilapil, a Nulud, a de la Rosa, an Espeleta who was Bishop of Cebu and acting Governor General and President of this Royal Audiencia.

Although it was not signed, everybody knew Father Burgos was its author. Only one who had experienced the points it discussed could have written so forcefully and correctly. And unlike the friars who emphasized the human weaknesses of the Filipino priests, the writer limited himself to objective issues and never descended to personal attacks.

In 1869, Carlos María de la Torre arrived as the new governor general of the Philippines. He immediately made known his liberal views, and in July that year, prominent Manileños serenaded him. One of those who joined in the public manifestation of support for liberalism was Father Burgos.

In the same year, the procurator in Madrid for the Philippine Franciscans, Fray Joaquín de Coria, published a series of unmitigated attacks on the Filipino clergy. There was nothing new in his writing, for he merely repeated the same charges of their alleged immorality, questionable loyalty to the government, and theological ineptitude. Burgos answered Coriás articles in the same newspaper, *La Discusión*.

Neither did Burgos offer new arguments. But his writings brought him before the public eye, and the Manila officials began to take note of him. Governor de la Torre, for example, ordered that his mail be censored.

With the change of ministries in Spain, Rafael Izquierdo was sent as the new governor general of the Philippines. Like his predecessor, he was known as a liberal in Spain—but a conservative in the Philippines.

When he arrived in Manila, rumors of secret meetings in the city and nearby places were rife, but Izquierdo gave little importance to them. Beyond ordering greater vigilance, or arresting suspects, he did practically nothing. Then, at about three o'clock in the early morning of 21 January 1872, he was roused from sleep by an emergency call that a mutiny had erupted at Fort San Felipe in Cavite the evening before. He immediately sent reenforcements and ordered that the full power of the law be applied on the guilty.

The reenforcements reached Cavite before noon of the same day, 21 January, and they immediately engaged the enemy. Next morning, at about seven o'clock, 22 January, the white flag of surrender appeared over the ramparts. Two hours later, a telegram reached the governor requesting that Father Burgos be arrested "for the good of the service." Actually, together with several others—Fr. Jacinto Zamora, Fr. Mariano Gómez, Feliciano Gómez (Father Mariano's nephew), Joaquín Pardo de Tavera (law professor at the University of Santo Tomás), Antonio María Regidor—he had already been apprehended the previous day. Shortly before noon, another telegram announced that the commander of the government troops, his job done, was leaving Cavite. The Cavite Mutiny lasted only from late 20 January to early 22 January 1872.

Several military trials were held immediately after. The most important, perhaps, was that of the three priests implicated in the mutiny. We no longer have the trial records, but we do know they were convicted and sentenced to die by *garrote vil*. The governor general asked to have them defrocked, but the archbishop of Manila asked to see the documents first before acceding to the request. These were not shown, and the archbishop saw no reason for degrading the condemned priests. And so, Frs. José Burgos, Mariano Gómez, and Jacinto Zamora were executed as priests in good standing on 17 February 1872, a little more than a month after the mutiny.

It seems that the mutineers who had been captured and interrogated by the military implicated the three priests. A certain Octavo, for example, testified that one Francisco Zaldúa had gone to Cavite to recruit volunteers to join the mutiny, with a promise of promotion and an increase in their salaries. He also assured them that the aim was to kill all the Spaniards, after which they would set up an independent Philippines. Father Burgos was going to be the head, until the Filipinos elected a permanent king.

Historians today believe the execution of the three priests was unjust. None of those who had testified against them had had contact with any of the priests, and their testimony was mere hearsay. Rather, the plot seems to have been concocted by Zaldúa . He was, however, one of the first to be executed, and so there was no way of disproving the statements of those interrogated. About a year later, the Supreme Military Council in Madrid, the highest Spanish military tribunal, disapproved the trials that followed the Cavite Mutiny and warned the governor general in Manila that such conduct by government officials violated the law and should not be repeated.

## José Rizal Mercado Y Alonso

In 1889, Rizal wrote a close friend that had it not been for the GOMBURZA executions (as the executions of Fathers Gómez, Burgos, and Zamora have come to be known), he would have become a Jesuit. He would not have written *Noli me tangere,* but a different book.

Rizal was born on 19 June 1861 to a prominent and cultured family in Calamba, Laguna. His father, Don Francisco Mercado, was a sugar planter on land leased from the Dominicans; he was a Chinese mestizo, had graduated from the College of San José. His mother, Teodora Alonso, was a well-read cultured lady, a graduate of the Colegio de Santa Rosa in Manila. Paciano, the hero's older brother, also studied at San José and was a close collaborator of Father Burgos. His seven sisters studied at the girls' schools in Manila.

Pepe, as Rizal was affectionately called, was the younger of two sons, apparently the favorite child. His mother taught him to read and write, and after a year at the elementary school in Biñan, Laguna, he transferred to the Ateneo Municipal administered by the Jesuits in Manila. He was only eleven years old at the time. Just before his execution on 30 December 1896, he recalled that his happiest days had been spent at the Ateneo, where

> by dint of studying, of analyzing myself, of reaching out for higher things, and of a thousand corrections, I was being transformed little by little, thanks to the influence of a beneficent professor. . . . Cultivating poetry and rhetoric had elevated my feelings, and Virgil, Cicero, and other authors showed me a new path which I could take.

He graduated in 1877 and continued for two years at the College of Medicine in the University of Santo Tomás. However, Rizal did not finish his training at Santo Tomás, for in 1882, he secretly sailed to Spain. But before that, he had already won prizes in two literary contests: in 1879, the first prize for his ode, *A la juventud filipina*, and in 1880, for his *El Consejo de los dioses*. In these writings, Rizal's love of country was already noticeable.

His arrival in Spain led to the organization of the Filipinos there. Soon they were publishing their own fortnightly, *La Solidaridad*, edited at first by Graciano López Jaena, and later by Marcelo H. del Pilar. But Rizal's most important work was the novel, *Noli me tangere*, which was printed in Berlin in 1887.

The novel tells about Crisóstomo Ibarra (shortened from Eibarramundi), a Filipino who comes home after years of study in Europe. In trying to uncover the mystery of his father's death, Ibarra comes face to face with an extreme situation of evil and corruption very painful to correct. That is why Rizal chose as title *Noli me tangere*, "Do Not Touch Me."

Ibarra, the hero of the novel, soon discovers that the friars were responsible for his father's death. Instead of seeking revenge, he decides to do good deeds for the people, because he is convinced that would have been his dead father's wish. But he is opposed by everyone. He manages to overcome the difficulties, until the parish priest concocts a "revolution" implicating him as the leader. Ibarra is jailed in Manila but escapes with the help of Elías.

The novel ends mysteriously, but with a faint glimmer of hope. Four years later, in 1891, Rizal's second novel, *El Filibusterismo*, came off the press in Ghent, Belgium. In this book, Ibarra returns, disguised as a jeweler, Simoun. Using his immense wealth, Simoun schemes to destroy the government by violent means. He wins over young students who have their own scores to settle with the abusive officialdom. But Simoun's plan fails, and he commits suicide.

Rizal's message was clear: there was widespread corruption in the Philippines, but violence and bloodshed were not the solution.

Rizal's writings inspired his countrymen. But they were misinterpreted by friars and officials in control of the government—and perhaps even by some of his own countrymen. Rizal insisted that both Spaniards and Filipinos needed to reform themselves: if they wanted to live in a free and just society, the Filipinos needed to learn to live in harmony with one another, each one performing his duties to the best of his abilities.

The Spaniards, too, needed to reform themselves. The government, on the other hand, should grant Philippine representation in the Cortes, or Spanish legislature, as well as the traditional freedoms of modern democracy: freedom of speech, of conscience, and of assembly. Filipinos, too, if they were worthy, should be appointed to government posts in their own country. Friars could continue in the Philippines, but they should not enjoy political authority.

Rizal was not read by all the Filipinos because less than 10 percent of the population knew Spanish. But his writings influenced important individuals; and during the trials immediately after Bonifacio's uprising exploded in August 1896, his name was continually mentioned. The government concluded that Rizal was the mastermind behind the whole revolutionary plot and sentenced him to die by firing squad. As the court declared, his writings served as strong propaganda

exerted on the ignorant and the credulous masses whom Rizal has, as it were, hypnotized. The adequate and necessary cause of the rebellion . . . Rizal did what the revolutionary leaders have done. He promoted the rebellion without determining precisely when it was to break out; it matters little, after all, whether it did so earlier or later. The main thing is that it was the result of a work deliberately undertaken; a tree which bore fruit sooner than was expected.

On 30 December 1896, a military squad escorted a man in a black suit out of a cell in Fort Santiago and led him to an open field outside the city walls. Then, in the presence of an awed crowd, the picket aimed their guns at him and fired. The man in black swayed a little and then turned around, falling with his face to the sky. Rizal, only thirty-five years of age, fell on that place then called Bagumbayan or "New Land" (now Luneta or Rizal Park). His executioners did not realize it then, but his death signaled the birth of a new land.

## Marcelo Hilario del Pilar

Marcelo H. del Pilar was the second principal figure in the propaganda movement in Spain. A Bulakeño born in 1850, he was a lawyer and worked as a defense attorney. In 1882, he founded the first bilingual newspaper in the Philippines, *Diariong Tagalo*. Rizal's article titled "Patriotism" appeared in its first issue.

Unlike Rizal, del Pilar was a man of action. Convinced that reforms would never be introduced unless the friars were expelled from the country, his objective was, first, to make the people lose respect for them, and then, decatholicize his country. This explains the series of activities he led before he sailed for Spain in October 1888.

Del Pilar made good use of his ability to speak and write in Tagalog, and composed a number of antifriar pamphlets. One of them was a parody of the Christian Decalogue. For example, instead of the first commandment, he wrote, "Worship the friar above all things." Instead of the fifth, he wrote, "Thou shalt not die without having money for the funeral." More trenchant was his version of the prayer, "Our Father," the first part of which reads:

> Our step-father who art in the convento, cursed be thy name, thy greed be far from us, thy throat be cut on earth as it is in heaven.

His most spectacular plan occurred on 1 March 1888. At his suggestion, the gobernadorcillos and barangay heads marched around the streets of Manila before seeking an audience with the governor general. They wanted to present a written demand to expel the friars and the archbishop of Manila. To their surprise, not only conservatives but also liberals in the city, with a very few exceptions, unanimously stood by the friars and the archbishop.

Not much later, Emilio Terrero (1885–1888) was succeeded by the more decisive Valeriano Weyler (1888–1891) as governor general of the Philippines. Warned, del Pilar left the Philippines in October 1888 and arrived in Spain in January 1889. He was sent there as the representative of the Manila-based Comité de Propaganda.

Del Pilar soon founded the fortnightly *La Solidaridad*, whose first issue appeared on 15 September 1889. Its purpose was to support liberal ideas and help "make democracy prevail among all the peoples both of the Peninsula and of the overseas provinces" of Spain.

The articles were serious essays by capable writers, like Rizal, and the Austrian ethnologist, Ferdinand Blumentritt. Blumentritt later became

Rizal's closest friend and adviser, whose opinions he always asked before making any serious decision. *La Solidaridad* usually discussed three topics: the Spanish colonial government, the friars, and reforms needed in the Philippines.

The first issues of *La Solidaridad* sold well, and José María Basa, exiled in Hong Kong after the Cavite Mutiny, smuggled copies into Manila. But after the fourth issue, the government became more vigilant and it was harder to bring the newspaper into the country.

The newspaper helped to focus the propaganda movement better. Del Pilar planned to start with a peaceful, legal campaign in Spain for reforms. This would last for two or three years, after which, hopefully having won the basic freedoms, they would return to the Philippines to continue the struggle. It was unclear whether the struggle would be peaceful, or through the use of arms.

## Suggestions for Further Reading

*(Complete information on recommended readings appears in the bibliography at the end of the book.)*

Arcilla, José S., "Documents concerning the Calamba deportations of 1891," *PS* 18; Arcilla, José S., *Understanding the Noli: Its historical context and literary influences;* Bernad, Miguel A., *Rizal and Spain: An essay in biographical context;* Cushner, Nicholas P., and John N. Schumacher, "Burgos and the Cavite Mutiny," *PS* 17; Guerrero, Leon Ma., *The first Filipino: A biography of José Rizal;* Schumacher, John N., *The making of a nation;* Schumacher, John N., *Father José Burgos, priest and nationalist;* Schumacher, John N., *The Propaganda Movement: 1880–1895;* Tormo Sanz, Leandro, *1872.,* tr. Antonio M. Molina; Villaroel, Fidel, *Father José Burgos, university student;* Villaroel, Fidel, *José Rizal and the University of Santo Tomás.*

# 11

## THE PHILIPPINE REVOLUTION

### Failure of the Propaganda Movement

Besides campaigning for peaceful reforms through books and newspapers, the Filipino propagandists in Spain linked themselves to the leaders of Spanish society. They hoped that by interesting politicians in their cause, the latter would introduce the appropriate reforms in the Cortes. They also hoped other friends who were not politicians, especially newspaper writers, would publicize their cause.

Nothing substantial resulted from their efforts. Spanish politicians seemed to support Filipino reform programs as long as their own political careers in Spain were not affected. Information on the Philippines did not interest the ordinary Spaniards and even antagonized them when the idea of separation was broached.

In 1890, Rizal learned of the ejection of his family and others from Calamba, allegedly for not paying the rental fees to the Dominicans who owned the land they occupied. Deeply disturbed, Rizal appealed the case to the higher tribunal in Spain, but it was denied and the decision of the lower court in the Philippines was sustained. Bitterly, Rizal wrote that one could never hope for justice from Spain. And he decided to return home. He had already stopped writing for *La Solidaridad*, alleging he was busy finishing a sequel to the *Noli me tangere*, after he had annotated Antonio de Morga's history of the Philippines published in 1605.

In September 1891, as mentioned, Rizal's second novel, *El Filibusterismo*, came off the press in Ghent, Belgium. A month later, convinced he had finished his task, he left Europe for good. As he had earlier explained to the Filipinos in Madrid,

If our countrymen hope in us here in Europe, they are mistaken. . . . The help we can give them is our lives in our country. The error all make in thinking we can help here, far away, is a great mistake indeed. The medicine must be brought near to the sick man. . . . The field of battle is the Philippines; that is where we should be.

With Rizal gone, it was a matter of time before the propaganda activity in Spain came to a stop. Stricter censorship in Manila had made it more difficult to smuggle in copies of La Solidaridad, funds had dwindled, and there were hardly any good writers for the paper. López Jaena had planned to go to Cuba and quit the paper, but he died in January 1896. Del Pilar bravely tried to continue, but soon Apolinario Mabini wrote him, asking him to close the newspaper. Del Pilar finally decided to leave Spain, unsure of whether to go to Japan or to the Philippines. But on 4 July 1896, he died in Barcelona.

Meanwhile, in Hong Kong, where Rizal was reunited with his family after leaving Europe, he continued thinking of the future of the Philippines. He began a third novel about Tagalog customs, but found it hard to write in Tagalog. He did not want to write it in Spanish because his intended readers (who, according to Rizal, "needed it most") did not know that language. He also planned to found a Filipino colony in Borneo, where he hoped they would enjoy freedom. But the Manila government refused permission, telling him it was more patriotic to develop the untapped natural resources of the Philippines.

And friends refused to leave Rizal in peace. They urged him to act as their leader, and for a short while, he seemed attracted to the idea of a revolution against the government. But Blumentritt dissuaded him from it, warning him not to burden his conscience with the blood of future innocent victims of violence.

Actually, Rizal had never favored the violent overthrow of the government. Simoun, the schemer in his second novel, wants to destroy Philippine society to build a new one. However, he fails; and instead of surrendering to the government, he commits suicide. And Rizal made the character of Father Fernández speak in the last chapter of El Filibusterismo against Simoun's use of evil means, a means bound to fail. Instead, Father Fernández exhorts,

We must win our freedom by deserving it, by improving the mind and enhancing the dignity of the individual, loving what is just, what is good, what is great, to the point of dying for it. When a people reaches these heights, God provides the weapon, and the idols and the tyrants fall like a house of cards, and freedom shines in the first dawn. Our misfortunes are our own fault, let us blame no one else for them. If Spain were to see us less tolerant of tyranny and readier to fight and suffer for our rights, Spain would be the first to give us our rights, Spain would be the first to give us freedom. . . . What is the use of independence if the slaves of today will be the tyrants of tomorrow?

As Rizal always maintained: Filipinos should prepare themselves for self-rule, before trying to govern themselves. To help them, he wrote rules for a "Philippine League" to train the Filipinos to live in unity, cooperation, and mutual help. Members of the future league were to be bound to secrecy. They were promised to give preference to fellow members when buying and selling, to aid any needy member, and neither to submit to any humiliation nor to treat anybody else in a disparaging manner. At each meeting, they were expected to bring some "work, some observation, some study, or a new member." A modest monthly contribution was demanded from each.

In other words, Rizal's attention was now directed to the Filipinos themselves. He felt it was a waste of time waiting for the government to do something for the people. Rather, the people must do something themselves.

Properly authorized, Rizal arrived in Manila on 26 June 1892. On 3 July, he organized his Philippine League in a house in Tondo owned by the Chinese mestizo, Ongjungco (some say Ongpingco). A large number of interested people were there at the inauguration of the society. Then, the blow fell.

Governor Eulogio Despujol confronted Rizal with some leaflets found in the baggage brought by his sister, Lucía, from Hong Kong. Titled "Poor Friars!" the materials were not really subversive, but were a diatribe against the church and the pope. Unable to explain its source, Rizal was arrested and tried three days later, and immediately exiled to Dapitan. Houses were searched, and other persons were also tried and shipped to other places in the Philippines. Those who held government positions were dismissed. And when Rizal left Manila, the Philippine League died.

## The Katipunan

One of those who had joined Rizal's league was Andrés Bonifacio, a warehouse worker, about thirty years old. He recruited others to the league, but the officers of the association found out to their horror that Bonifacio had been telling the new members that their purpose was to launch a violent revolution to topple the government.

When Rizal left, Bonifacio reorganized the league and helped establish several councils in Manila. But he was more than ever convinced only violent means would succeed in achieving change. Soon, the Supreme Council of the league dissolved itself. Some members regrouped themselves into a Cuerpo de Compromisarios, pledged to contribute monthly dues to continue the peaceful campaign in Spain. But the less schooled and the more radical sympathizers grouped around Bonifacio who now founded his own association, the Kataastaasang Kagalanggalang Katipunan ng mga Anak ng Bayan.

Necessarily, because of its purpose, the Katipunan had to be a secret society. Organized along Masonic lines, it had a supreme council (Kataastaasang Sanggunian) composed of a president, a fiscal, a secretary, a treasurer, and comptroller. There were provincial councils (Sanggunian Bayan) and town or popular councils (Sanggunian Balangay). Membership came mainly from the lower socioeconomic groups in Manila and nearby Tagalog areas.

Just like the Masons, they were sworn to secrecy. They signed their pledge with blood obtained by making an incision on their arm. They were grouped in three ranks. The lowest, the *katipun* (associate), used the password, *anak ng bayan*. The next, the *kawal* (soldier), had for a password, *Gom-bur-za*. And the highest, the *bayani* (patriot), used as their password *Rizal*. (As we shall see, this was later used by the military tribunal against the future national hero to condemn him to death as a revolutionary.) Each grade had its own insignia and specific colors. Until discarded because it was too cumbersome, the triangle system of membership was used: that is, a member recruited two others who did not know each other.

By 1895, three years after its founding, the movement had significantly spread. Bonifacio continued as the *supremo* or head of the Supreme Council. His close aide was Emilio Jacinto, a twenty-year-old law student, who provided some guidelines for the *katipuneros* in the *Kartilla ng Katipunan*. Some of its principles were:

1. A life not consecrated to a lofty and just purpose is like a tree which casts no shadow—a poisonous weed.
2. To do good for some personal motive and not because of a true desire to do good is not virtue.
3. Real saintliness consists in being charitable, in loving one's fellow men, and in adjusting one's every word, action, and deed to right and reason.
4. All men are equal, be the color of their skin black or white. One may be superior to another in wisdom, looks, or wealth, but they are equal as men.
5. Do not squander time; lost riches can be recovered; but time lost cannot be regained.
6. Think not of a woman as a thing with which to pass the time merely, but as a helper, as a partner in the hardships of life. Respect her in her weakness and think only of the mother who brought you into the world and took care of you in your childhood.

The Philippine Revolution    87

Great and noble is he who, although born in the forest with no knowledge except that of his own tongue, is possessed of good character, is true to his word and mindful of his dignity and honor; a man who does not oppress or help those who oppress; a man who loves and looks after the welfare of his country.

Preach and follow these doctrines.

In 1894, the Katipunan owned a printing press, with types either bought or stolen from the office of the newspaper, *Diario de Manila*. Jacinto edited a newspaper, *Kalayaan*, to serve as the mouthpiece of the association. To avoid detection, a false address was given. The first issue was supposedly printed in Yokohama, Japan, on 1 February 1896, under the editorship of Marcelo H. del Pilar.

Total membership of the Katipunan has been variously estimated, but it is pretty much agreed that by June 1896, everything seemed ready for action. A red flag with three K's had been adopted, a war plan had been finalized by Bonifacio and Jacinto, some arms and gunpowder had been stored, and money and supplies had been collected.

Meantime, rumors and reports of suspicious meetings at night had reached the government. On 13 August, the Augustinian friar of San Pedro Makati reported that anti-Spanish meetings were going on in his parish. Women, too, were holding their own gatherings.

Six days later, 19 August 1896, Teodoro Patiño visited his sister, Honoria, who was living in an orphanage in Mandaluyong. He wanted to take her away because he feared for her safety in case the revolution started. According to one version, Honoria started crying and the sister portress came in to find out what was wrong. Neither Honoria nor Teodoro could guard the secret of the Katipunan any longer. Alarmed, the sister convinced Teodoro to report the whole thing to the parish priest of Tondo, where he resided.

About six o'clock in the evening, Patiño went to see Fray Mariano Gil, the Augustinian curate of Tondo, who lost no time verifying the story. He rushed to the printing room of *Diario de Manila* and found the evidence: a lithographic stone with two blank receipts of the Katipunan in Tagalog, besides Tagalog copies of the society rules and other incriminating documents. Fray Gil proceeded to the authorities to present them with what he had found.

Suspects and accomplices were rounded up and jailed. Some barely escaped. Bonifacio and Jacinto were warned in time and went into hiding.

The discovery of the Katipunan left them no other choice but to openly revolt. On 26 August 1896, an important date in Philippine history,

Bonifacio ended a stormy meeting in Kalookan by taking out his cédula personal and tearing it to pieces before his followers. He was renouncing allegiance to Spain. Four days later, blood flowed: a violent revolution had begun.

## Revolution

The so-called Philippine Revolution was actually many revolutions put together. It started in Manila, and, at first, was confined to the immediate area around the city. Not all the Filipinos joined the antigovernment ranks, and Filipino volunteers against the rebels came from as far as Zamboanga. Not all the revolutionary leaders were against the friars. And when the latter were imprisoned in rebel camps, the people visited them, bringing them food and clothes.

The first phase of the revolution ended with the Pact of Biaknabato signed on 14 December 1897. But because not all the revolutionaries were in favor of the truce, sporadic fighting continued. Then, as we shall read more about in chapter 12, the Americans under then Commodore George Dewey destroyed the Spanish fleet in Manila Bay on 1 May 1898. Two-and-a-half months later, on 13 August, Manila fell to the Americans. There was still no peace, for on 4 February 1899, fighting between Filipinos and Americans began. Aguinaldo finally surrendered to the Americans in April 1901, but there were still pockets of anti-American resistance. The last of the intransigents, Miguel Malvar of Batangas, finally surrendered in 1907.

In August 1896, the first victims of the revolution were Chinese traders massacred by Filipino hotheads characterized by a traditional antipathy towards the Chinese. But by 30 August, disturbances occurred all over the city: an initial attack in Sampaloc was repulsed by civil guards; riots broke out in Pandacan; hand-to-hand fighting was reported in San Juan, east of Manila, where about 100 Filipinos were killed and twice that number taken as prisoners. Four of these prisoners were summarily sentenced and executed, together with fifty-four others. Two groups sailed down the Pasig and attacked the Spaniards and friars hiding in the Pasig church.

Next day, news came that some Cavite towns had fallen into rebel hands. On 3 September, General Mariano Llanera of the revolutionary forces attacked San Isidro, Nueva Ecija, but he retreated with the arrival of government volunteers from Pampanga.

Governor Ramón Blanco immediately cabled Spain for reenforcements. On 30 August, he declared a state of emergency in eight provinces:

Manila, Bulacan, Pampanga, Nueva Ecija, Tarlac, Laguna, Cavite, and Batangas. He announced a forty-eight-hour grace period during which the insurgents were called upon to surrender (and for which he was severely criticized).

The next months saw more bloodshed and government reprisals. Prominent people, perhaps unconnected with the revolution, were arrested. The prisons were congested, and many in Fort Santiago by the mouth of the Pasig either drowned or were suffocated when the tide came in from Manila Bay. On 4 September, four were shot in Bagumbayan; on 12 September, thirteen in Cavite; on 30 December, Rizal was shot; on 4 January 1897, eleven Bicolanos, including priests; on 11 January, thirteen more were executed; and on 23 March, nineteen were massacred in Panay. Neither were the rebels idle. They killed friars, at least thirteen Recollects and three Augustinians.

Bonifacio was not a soldier and he suffered defeats when he faced the Spanish lines. He lost the fight in San Juan del Monte, east of Manila; his line was scattered at Nangka river in Marikina; and at Balara he barely escaped with his life.

But in Cavite, Emilio Aguinaldo was winning. Noveleta, San Francisco de Malabon (today, General Trias), Naic, Magallanes, Alfonso, Silang, Imus—these fell to his troops. Finally, they occupied the Recollect estate in Imus, which became their base of operations.

Early in 1897, Governor Camilo Polavieja who had relieved Blanco, announced a policy of "summary retaliation." First, government units checked the Bulacan–Nueva Ecija line, forcing the rebels to retreat farther into the hills and forests of central Luzon. Many in Bulacan surrendered. By February, his three generals were concentrating on Cavite from three different positions: General Lachambre, on the Laguna-Batangas-Cavite front, to face Aguinaldo; General Galbis, to guard the area south of the Pasig river; and General Zappino, whose force consisted mainly of native volunteers, on the Manila-Morong (now Rizal province) front, to prevent General Llanera in the north from contacting Aguinaldo.

On 26 February, Zapote, Silang, and Dasmariñas had been taken by government troops. A month later, on 25 March, Imus fell.

In this interlude from January to March 1897, the rivalry between Bonifacio and Aguinaldo came to a head. In March 1897, the rebels agreed to form a revolutionary government in place of the Katipunan. But instead of Bonifacio, Aguinaldo was elected president, while Bonifacio was chosen as minister of the interior. Daniel Tirono objected to the choice of Bonifacio for the post, for which he thought the lawyer José del

Rosario was better suited by training. Bonifacio felt insulted, and stormed out of the meeting.

The next day, 23 March, Bonifacio summoned a second meeting, which the Aguinaldo group ignored. A court martial found him guilty of treason and imposed the death sentence on him. Aguinaldo commuted the sentence. On 10 May 1897, however, Mariano Noriel handed sealed orders to Lázaro Makapagal, commanding him to take Bonifacio and his brother to Mount Buntis, where he was ordered to shoot the two brothers. Until now, it is not clear who ordered the death of the founder of the Katipunan.

## Suggestions for Further Reading

*(Complete information on recommended readings appears in the bibliography at the end of the book.)*

Agoncillo, Teodoro A., *The revolt of the masses: The story of Bonifacio and the Katipunan;* Aguinaldo, Emilio, *Memoirs of the revolution,* tr. Luz Colendrino-Bucu; Aguinaldo, Emilio, "True account of the revolution," in García, Mauro (ed.), *Aguinaldo in retrospect.*

# 12

## AMERICAN INTERVENTION

### The Pact of Biaknabato

The last Cavite town finally fell to government troops on 14 May 1897, but Aguinaldo managed to escape to Biaknabato in Bulacan. There he regrouped his forces. He placed his military contingents under a unified command; a new flag was adopted (similar to the present one except that it had no rays around the sun); and a new cabinet was appointed.

From Biaknabato he issued several proclamations, the most important of which was a Philippine constitution. To last for two years, it carried fifty signatures and was promulgated on 1 November 1897. It emphasized three things: separation from Spain, a bill of rights, and a provision that the Philippines would be an independent republic.

Fighting continued in several places. The governor general wanted to end hostilities, and cabled to Spain for authorization to arrange a truce. He explained that even though he could crush the rebels, Spain would still not win the good will of the Filipinos. Fighting and bloodshed were doing more harm than good.

The first feelers were channeled through the Jesuit mission superior, Fr. Pío Pi. He was hesitant at first; but hoping things could be settled peacefully, he agreed to invite Aguinaldo to an initial parley at a place and date the latter would choose. Complaints could be aired and efforts would be made to satisfy their just demands.

Because Aguinaldo imposed conditions, the government backed off from the plan. But Pedro A. Paterno, who had once lived in Spain, did not give up. He volunteered to serve as liaison and effect a peaceful solution to the revolt. With authorization from Governor Primo de Rivera, he undertook several missions to Biaknabato, talked with Aguinaldo, and tried to convince the latter's advisers to accept the government peace proposals.

There were at least two preliminary pacts, before one was signed on 14 December 1897, which seemed to satisfy both parties. But today, historians disagree on what its actual provisions were.

However, it is certain that Primo de Rivera received authorization from his government to offer as much as 800,000 pesos to pay the rebels on condition that they lay down their arms and accept Spanish sovereignty. Reforms demanded by the rebels were not specified, for the Madrid government had authorized the governor general to introduce reforms only *after* peace returned.

One-half of the money was intended for Aguinaldo and his staff after they should have laid down their arms and taken the boat for Hong Kong. The other half would be given when the rest of the rebel forces laid down their arms too. But later, wary, with reason, lest the remaining 400,000 pesos be waylaid and not properly distributed, the government handed a check for only 200,000 pesos, while withholding the rest of the sum until all fighting should have ended.

On 29 December, two weeks after signing the pact, Aguinaldo and twenty-seven others boarded a boat in Sual, Pangasinan for Hong Kong. Two days later, Isabelo Artacho, Aguinaldo's secretary of the interior, called a meeting at Biaknabato to demand that at least 100,000 pesos be left to those who were staying behind. The understanding was that the money was to go to the men who had taken up arms, to be shared accordingly; to aid families ruined by war; to widows; and to those whose property had been embargoed. Apparently, that did not happen.

Aguinaldo later claimed he had given about 5,000 pesos to Artacho. But the rest of the money he kept. This was contrary to the pact of Biaknabato. But the rebels countered that the government for its part had failed in its promise and no reforms had been introduced. Neither did the rebels surrender their arms. The truce was meaningless from the start.

On 2 January 1898, Aguinaldo deposited the entire sum of 400,000 pesos in the Chartered Hongkong Bank in the name of Aguinaldo and Company, who claimed they represented a *soberanía interior* of the Philippines. This meant that, besides the "exterior" Spanish colonial government, there was a secret government in the Philippines. In other words, when Aguinaldo signed the pact of Biaknabato, he was already the head of an underground group, whose existence the truce neither ended nor recognized. Besides, the act of depositing the entire money was not in accordance with the terms of the pact. Apparently, the Filipino exiles to Hong Kong had no intention of honoring their signature.

On 13 April, Aguinaldo received a court summons to answer charges filed by Isabelo Artacho. He had arrived from the Philippines to claim his share of the money, and demanded an accounting of how it was being spent. Aguinaldo escaped incognito to Singapore. There, he met a man whose fertile imagination changed the course of Philippine history—Howard Bray.

Bray was an English trader who wrote about the Philippines in a Singapore newspaper. His business sense told him he had an opportunity perhaps to make some extra money. He sought out Aguinaldo who tried to hide his identity, and finally succeeded in arranging an interview between the Filipino rebel leader and the United States consul in Singapore, E. Spencer Pratt.

We shall never know what ideas were exchanged between a rebel leader who did not know English, and an American state official who did not know Spanish. Bray served as their interpreter, but a scholar described him as having "talked too much." Later, against the consul's denials, Aguinaldo claimed Pratt had promised the United States government would recognize the future independence of the Philippines.

On 26 April, Pratt cabled Commodore George Dewey in Hong Kong about Aguinaldo. Earlier, Dewey had been sent there by the American government as a military precaution, and he was about to sail to the Philippines when the message reached him. He merely answered with instructions to have Aguinaldo return to Hong Kong, and did not bother to wait for the latter. Aguinaldo was not important to his plans.

## The End of the Spanish Regime

While these things were happening in the Philippines, Cuba, another Spanish colony, was also fighting for independence. Because American capital had been invested in the island, there was pressure on the Washington government to intervene. On 15 February 1898, the American USS *Maine*, sent on a "friendly visit" to the island, was mysteriously blown up. American public opinion immediately condemned Spain, even before investigations had been finished. After a thorough reexamination of the evidence, Admiral Hyman G. Rickover of the U.S. Navy concluded in 1976 that the explosion had been due to spontaneous combustion in a coal bunker, and Spain was no more to blame than the United States.

But emotions had been stirred up. Without proper authorization, Undersecretary of the Navy Theodore Roosevelt ordered Dewey to Hong Kong, and while there, to keep his fleet in battle alert. Lest the newspapers sensationalize the incident, Secretary John D. Long did not countermand his subordinate's order. Not much later, the U.S. Congress, ostensibly to liberate the Cubans "groaning" under the yoke of Spanish tyranny, declared war against Spain on 25 April, retroactive to 21 April. Six days later, Dewey steamed off Mirs Bay near Hong Kong, and headed for Manila.

At about five o'clock in the morning of 1 May 1898, Dewey's boats sighted the Spanish fleet at anchor off Cavite. Maneuvering closer, they opened fire, and in less than three hours, without any serious counterfire, destroyed the Spanish fleet.

Had Dewey left after fulfilling his mission, things would have been different. But like any good military leader, he stayed on, following the basic fighting axiom which says that every military victory must be consolidated lest the enemy regroup and hit back. That is why, before leaving Hong Kong, he cabled his home government for reenforcements. Now after his unexpectedly easy victory, he awaited them. And on 4 May, he received word they were on the way.

Meanwhile, on 19 May, Aguinaldo returned to the Philippines aboard an American boat. He did not go ashore immediately, but stayed overnight aboard ship. He finally had a talk with Dewey and, the next morning, was rowed ashore, and proceeded to the former Spanish governor's residence in Cavite which he made his headquarters.

This is the second mystery in Aguinaldo's career. He claimed the American naval commander promised him independence, but the latter always denied he had said anything that could be interpreted in that sense. But he admitted that, since they were fighting a common enemy, the Filipinos could be useful to harass the Spaniards on land, while the Americans would do their bit on the sea.

Dewey hoped he would not have to use guns to force the Spaniards to yield. But the Spanish military code forbade easy surrender. Court martial awaited the guilty. Besides, the Spaniards were aware that the Filipinos had resumed hostilities against them. Lest the Filipinos enter and sack the city, they demanded "protection" from the Americans, who had claimed military victory over them. But if the Americans agreed, they risked alienating the Filipinos whom they wanted to use against the Spaniards.

The first American troops arrived in the Philippines on 30 June, and by 7 August, negotiations were in full swing. Dewey pressed for evacuation of the noncombatants and the surrender of the city within forty-eight hours. The governor general pointed out it would be impossible since the Filipinos had surrounded the city. Furthermore, he needed his government's authorization from Madrid to do so.

Finally, it was agreed that to save Spanish military honor, there would be a token fight, but the white flag would immediately be raised to avoid useless shooting.

At 5:30 at dawn on 13 August 1898, the Americans, together with the Tagalog forces, began firing. For about an hour there was gunfire, but it accomplished nothing. Then from their boats, the Americans bombarded Fort San Antonio Abad south of Manila (that is, Intramuros). An hour before noon that day, gunfire from the ships ceased altogether as the white flag of surrender appeared above the walls of the city. At six o'clock that evening, the Spanish flag above Fort Santiago was taken down, and in its place the American Stars and Stripes was hoisted.

The Americans had conquered. After 327 years, Spain finally lost her colony in the Southeast Asia, while the new republican colossus of the new world had acquired its first colony. The United States of America had become a colonizer.

## The Americans Decide to Keep the Philippines

When the Americans destroyed the Spanish fleet in May, they had not expressed any intention of departing from their democratic traditions and becoming a colonizing power. But American victory over Spain, till then considered one of the European powers, occasioned a national feeling of expansion and optimism. They had, unfortunately, no plans for their new colony.

Neither did William McKinley, the American president, know what to do with the Philippines. He later said that at first, he thought of keeping only part of the country. But what about the rest of the country? Should the Philippines, instead, be abandoned, perhaps returned to Spain, or maybe given to the Filipinos to rule by themselves? This would have provoked international problems. Nations would have elbowed one another to grab all or part of the archipelago. The possibility of selling the country to the highest bidder was just as problematical.

To McKinley, then, the only "decent" solution was to keep the entire Philippine archipelago. By September 1898, he cabled the American panel at the peace conference in Paris to demand the entire Philippines. There was some hedging about, but finally Spain agreed to the Treaty of Paris which transferred jurisdiction over the Philippines to the United States of America.

Signed 8 December 1898, the treaty provided that Spain would receive $20 million as indemnity for the war and the unfinished building projects in the Philippines. The Filipinos would be granted religious freedom and, subject to approval by the American Congress, civil rights.

To obtain information about the Philippines, the Schurman Commission (so called because it was headed by Jacob G. Schurman) was sent to the country in January 1899. It arrived in March, a month after fighting between the Americans and the Filipinos had broken out.

Besides seeking data, the Commission assured the Filipinos that the United States aimed at "the well-being, the prosperity, and the happiness of the Philippine people, and their elevation and advancement to a position among the most civilized peoples of the world." To carry this out, the Filipinos had to accept American sovereignty first. There was nothing wrong in this, the Americans added, for their government was "more solicitous to spread peace and happiness . . . freedom . . . and self-government."

These words were not necessarily believed, or every liked, by all the Filipinos. The Aguinaldo group, for example, threatened those who welcomed the Americans. As a result, only members of the ilustrado class volunteered information to the Commission, while the ordinary people stayed away. Hence, initial knowledge about the Philippines was supplied by a small group of the elite. Consequently, the first decisions of the American government regarding the Filipinos were based on rather limited information.

On 4 May 1899, the Schurman Commission suggested that a governor general be appointed to rule the Philippines. An advisory group to help him should be elected at large, but the governor should enjoy absolute right of veto. An independent judiciary was also recommended.

More importantly, the commission urged that the Americans stay in the Philippines permanently. There was no Philippine nation, but only a "collection of tribes," it argued. There was no public opinion, which a true democracy needed, and the Filipinos could not rule themselves properly.

A second commission was appointed, this time to implement the Schurman plan for the Philippines. Called the Taft Commission (headed by William H. Taft), it arrived in 1900, and assumed legislative powers. By June 1901, a civil government was established and Taft himself became the first civil governor of the Philippines. The members of the cabinet were: Dean C. Worcester, secretary of the interior; Henry C. Ide, secretary of finance; Luke E. Wright, secretary of commerce and police; Bernard Moses, secretary of public instruction. Some Filipinos were also appointed: Cayetano Arellano, chief justice of the Supreme Court; Trinidad Pardo de Tavera, Benito Legarda, and José R. de Luzurriaga, nonvoting members of the commission; and Felipe Buencamino, director of the Bureau of Civil Service.

By November 1900, less than two years after the start of the Filipino-American fighting, a significant number of Filipinos had become convinced of the futility of resisting the Americans. Thinking themselves to be no less patriotic than those fighting with their guns, they believed patriotism had to be tempered with the painful truth that the Americans were militarily superior. There would be more benefits from peaceful coexistence with the Americans: For example, two years previously, on 18 August 1898, just five days after the fall of Manila, banks and commercial houses had reopened. In September 1898, schools, too, reopened, with Fr. William McKinnon, Roman Catholic chaplain of the California Volunteers, as the first city superintendent of schools.

Finally, in towns where peace had returned, an American-style municipal government was established. Popular elections were held for the town president, vice-president, and members of the town council. Soon a Municipal Code was promulgated, by which the town president, with the approval of the town council, appointed the town treasurer and the secretary. Besides, the councillors enjoyed delegated authority to collect taxes, manage the town's public property, and supervise the construction of local public edifices.

Little by little, the Filipinos were being accustomed to the American style of democratic government.

### Suggestions for Futher Reading

*(Complete information on recommended readings appears in the bibliography at the end of the book.)*

De Jesús, Edilberto, Jr., "Aguinaldo and the Americans," *Philippine Historical Review* 1; Le Roy, James A., *The Americans in the Philippines* (2 vols.); Reuter, Frank T., *Catholic influence on American colonial policies, 1898–1904;* Robinson, John L., "The history of acquisition: Foundations for misunderstanding," *PS* 14; Stanley, Peter W., *A nation in the making;* U.S. Philippine Commission, *Reports of the Philippine Commission (1900; 1901).*

# 13

## REORGANIZING THE PHILIPPINES

### Philippine Independence

Although he was back in the Philippines on 19 May 1898, Aguinaldo was rowed ashore by the Americans only the next morning. With Dewey's permission, he occupied the former residence of the Cavite governor, and began to recruit men to resume the fight against the Spaniards.

The third day after his return, 21 May, Aguinaldo called on the Filipinos to rise in arms, since, he added, their "hour of liberation" had come. Three days later, he assumed dictatorial powers. Soon he learned that arms were arriving from Hong Kong, and that American reenforcements were on their way. As a precaution against any eventuality, he decided to seek recognition of an independent Philippine nation. But since no independent Philippines existed, Aguinaldo had to create one.

News of several rebel successes against the Spaniards encouraged Aguinaldo to act immediately. On 12 June 1898, a Sunday, "Dictator" Aguinaldo proclaimed the independence of a new Philippine republic, with its own flag (sewn by Mrs. Felipe Agoncillo) and its own national anthem (composed by Julián Felipe):

There can now be proclaimed before the Filipino people and the civilized nations its only aspiration, namely, the independence of the country, which proclamation should not be delayed for any ulterior objects of this government.

Strange as it may seem, there was no "Act" of independence read or proclaimed that day. Aguinaldo wanted such proclamation to take place *after* the towns and provinces had been reorganized. But the ceremonies on 12 June signified in Aguinaldo's eyes the birth a new nation. Dewey had been invited, but he did not attend. He did not want to legitimize or even create the impression that he recognized the independence of the Philippines.

On 20 June, forty-five laws written in Tagalog were promulgated to reorganize the town and provincial administrative systems. On 23 June, a "revolutionary government" took the place of the dictatorship. A cabinet of four secretaries was set up: that of war, of public works, of police, and of education.

On 15 July the cabinet secretaries were named. Finally, on 1 August, an Act of Independence was promulgated, as if to formalize what to Aguinaldo and his followers was already a reality since 12 June.

The first American troops sent to the Philippines had landed in Cavite on 30 June, and Aguinaldo was asked to vacate the area. When more Americans later landed in Parañaque, the Filipinos again gave way to them. Mainly because of insufficient arms, Aguinaldo kept yielding to American demands. But he ordered passive resistance, while relaying information on the American movements to the Spaniards. And when the Americans entered Manila on 13 August, the Filipinos followed them and looted the city. Because of this they were later barred from entering Manila. Aguinaldo asked for, but was refused, the use of the churches for his troops, and the Spanish governor's residence or the Malacañan Palace for his headquarters.

This was the root of the hostility between the Filipinos and the Americans. Before Manila fell, Aguinaldo had already made his people believe they had won their independence. But no other nation recognized the Philippines as a sovereign nation. On the other hand, the American consul in Manila cabled his government on 6 September, three months later, that a delegation of 4,000 Visayan soldiers representing business interests had pledged their loyalty if the Philippines was annexed to the United States. This means that, even among the Filipinos, Aguinaldo's plan was either ignored or not accepted. For their part, the Americans considered the Philippines a colony they had won from Spain in a war.

On 4 July 1898, Aguinaldo moved his capital to Bacoor, from where he issued decrees most probably drafted by his closest adviser, Apolinario Mabini. In September, he transferred the seat of his government to Bulacan and there, on 15 September 1898, the Malolos Congress opened to draft a constitution.

After several months, a constitution based on the Spanish and South American models (except the preamble which was literally copied from that of the United States constitution) was approved. It provided for the separation of the executive, judicial, and legislative powers of government. An elected president was granted absolute veto power that a two-thirds vote of the legislature might override. After a heated debate decided by only one vote, the delegates approved the separation of church and state in the future republic.

The constitution was never implemented, for on 4 February 1899, fighting erupted between the Filipinos and the Americans. But Filipino political leadership never hesitated to act as though their country were truly a sovereign nation, even if still unrecognized by the family of nations.

## War, or Insurrection?

Both Spain and the United States considered the Philippines a colony. No amount of protest, therefore, gave the latter any right to be represented by Felipe Agoncillo in the Paris peace talks of 1898.

But because of its democratic tradition, the United States claimed it was not colonizing the Philippines in the traditional way. Rather, they were "benevolently assimilating" the archipelago to "train" the Filipinos in self-rule as a preparation for eventual independence.

This was precisely the problem. The Filipinos claimed they could already govern themselves and exist as a sovereign nation. The Americans disagreed. Who was right? The search for an answer led to armed conflict.

Early on, Aguinaldo had felt the Americans had come not as liberators but as the new masters of his country. He had not been invited to the conferences before the fall of Manila. And when Filipino fighters were banned from entering the city when it fell, his worst fears were proven right.

Between August 1898 and February 1899, both sides kept provoking each other. Each group had been assigned exclusive zones, but neither of them observed the boundary lines. Filipinos kept entering unoccupied American zones, while American military engineers crossed Filipino lines. American correspondents also went behind Filipino lines to take pictures.

On 2 February 1899, American military engineers were detained by the Filipinos and released only on vigorous complaint by Gen. Elwell S. Otis, the American commander.

Two nights later, 4 February, at about eight o'clock, four Filipinos crossed the American line, despite the sentry's warning. Because they ignored the command to stop, the sentry fired on them, for he had received peremptory orders to fire if his post was invaded. A number of the Filipinos were hit. General firing followed.

Next day, American troops broke the Filipino line at San Juan del Monte, east of Manila, and occupied the zone around Tondo, north of the Pasig. One after the other, they took Marikina, Santa Ana, and San Pedro Makati. After two days, the Americans lost 234 men, while the Filipinos left more than 500 fighters buried in their own trenches, with at least 200 taken as prisoners.

Because the Americans had no integrated strategy, it was not too easy for them, despite superior weapons, to subdue the Filipinos. But the outcome was not much in doubt.

By mid-February 1899, Iloilo, which had never accepted the Aguinaldo government, accepted American sovereignty. After Iloilo, Cebu fell, and in early July, the Sulu sultanate signed a treaty of friendship with the American authorities.

Fresh reenforcements drove the Filipinos farther north of Luzon. On 31 March, Malolos fell; eight months later, 12 November, Tarlac. The Filipinos dispersed to adopt guerrilla tactics. In one of the skirmishes, Aguinaldo was almost killed had it not been for the young Gregorio del Pilar who died at Tirad Pass. The Filipino rebel leader escaped to Palanan, Isabela. From this time on, the American campaign centered on capturing him.

One day, Aguinaldo's courier from Palanan was captured, his message was decoded, and Gen. Frederick Funston hit on a plan to capture Aguinaldo. Pretending to be captured prisoners of Macabebe auxiliaries disguised as insurgent troops that Aguinaldo had sent for, the Americans reached Aguinaldo's secret hideout in Isabela. There, at a signal, the Americans opened fire, and Aguinaldo yielded. He was taken to Manila, kept at Malacañan Palace for a few days. Finally, on 19 April 1901, he took the oath of allegiance to the United States government. He called on his followers to lay down their arms, and explained that at that moment his love and service for his country demanded that he accept American sovereignty.

The center of resistance was broken. There still remained pockets of stubborn anti-Americanism, which some historians classify as outright banditry.

Fighting lasted about two years. With the return of peace, civil government was established, American troops were reduced, and Filipinos were coopted as Philippine Scouts, under American officers, into the permanent military force in the Philippines.

More importantly (although the old Spanish civil and criminal codes continued in force as much as possible under American law), the American-style of democratic government was introduced to the Filipinos. For lack of American civilian personnel, the American soldiers assumed civilian tasks in the government, the police, the treasury, the schools, etc. It was by this combination of "schoolbooks and krags" that the Americans slowly won over the majority of the Filipinos. Finally, the remaining Spanish officials and military officers were recalled and repatriated to Spain. The Filipinos took their places until Americans came and replaced them.

## Educating the Filipinos

The American impression that there was no Philippine nation but only a "collection of tribes" might have been exaggerated. But some data seem to support the view.

Population in 1900 was estimated at 7.6 million, of whom 6.9 million were listed as "civilized Christians." The rest were what are called today the "cultural minorities." There were thirty-nine civil provinces and nine military commandancies or areas not fully conquered and effectively ruled by the central government. There was only one city, Manila. Of the 7,102 islands comprising the archipelago, only 342 were inhabited.

Literacy was low. Newspapers had a circulation of 46,454, or an average of 1,858 copies of each publication. Not only that; in the archipelago there were only twelve libraries, holding only 4,029 books, or an average of 335 in each. And of the young Filipinos of school age (ten years or older), more than one-half were illiterate.

Besides the political reorganization, then, the Americans immediately introduced a system of free primary education. By April 1900, there were about 1,000 schools in the Philippines, 39 of them in Manila. Unfortunately, average daily attendance at school was between 4,000 and 5,000 pupils, a very low number compared to the 4.9 million Filipino children of school age.

Because there were not enough books in Spanish, and none at all in any of the Philippine languages, American textbooks were used. The medium of instruction, then, for practical reasons had to be English. The Americans also hoped English would unite the people into one strong state.

As mentioned, some of the American military served as the first teachers. But in 1901, volunteer teachers from the United States arrived: 48 aboard the *Sheridan*, 48 aboard the *Buford*, and 523 aboard the *Thomas*. That is why the first American teachers in the Philippines have been called the "Thomasites."

But there were problems. Was religion, as in the Spanish regime, to continue as a school subject? Some wanted it removed, because they claimed it would revive the difficulties the Filipinos had taken up arms to solve. But Governor Taft pointed out that the Treaty of Paris provided that Filipino customs and traditions should be respected, and religion was an essential factor in Filipino culture. A compromise solution was approved, and religion would be taught to children whose parents asked for it, thrice weekly, and outside of class hours.

This was perhaps a serious blunder. American democracy protected the separation of church and state. But without formal religious instruction in the schools, a generation of Filipinos soon grew up indifferent to morality and personal integrity. Corruption in public office can be traced to this lack.

Another problem was the lack of funds. In the school year 1903–1904, to accommodate as many pupils in the schools as possible but without adding extra facilities, the primary school was shortened from four to only three years. In 1904–1905, it was decided that only Americans could teach in the upper intermediate grades, while Filipinos were assigned to the lower primary grades.

The most serious difficulty was the lack of a clear program of education. Besides training in citizenship, the program of education of 1903 aimed at producing an "educated peasantry." It was thought that unless the rural folk could read and write, they would always be abused by the caciques and the powerful but small group of rich people. Six years later, the program was changed to stress "practical training." Ideally, it was hoped that by Grade Three the pupil would be able to produce salable items, and by Grade Four, earn a living.

This frequent change of policies was harmful. Experts say that a child needs a minimum of four years to be able to retain what is taught. But instead of continuing the same matter for such time as was necessary to absorb it, something new was always added. And, for one reason or another, as they went on from grade to grade, more and more children left school without finishing the minimum of four years in primary school. Hence, many remained as illiterate as before.

And yet the Philippine school system then was better than that in other colonial countries at that time. In 1907, 7 percent of Filipino children of school age were attending school, but only 1 percent in India. The majority of the Filipinos learned English, and in due time, some became poets and prose writers recognized all over the world.

## Suggestions for Further Reading

*(Complete information on recommended readings appears in the bibliography at the end of the book.)*

Bain, David H., *Sitting in darkness: Americans in the Philippines;* Gates, John M., *Schoolbooks and krags: The United States Army in the Philippines, 1898–1902;* Linn, Brian M., *The U. S. Army and counterinsurgency in the Philippine War, 1899–1902;* May, Glenn Anthony, "Filipino resistance to American occupation: Batangas, 1899–1902," *PHR* 48; May, Glenn Anthony, "The zones of Batangas," *PS* 29; Pier, Arthur S., *American apostles to the Philippines;* Salamanca, Bonifacio S., *The Filipino reaction to American rule, 1901–1913;* Scott, William H., *Ilocano responses to American aggression, 1900–1901;* Taylor, John R. M., *The Philippine insurrection against the United States. A compilation of documents with notes and introduction;* Welch, Richard E., *Response to imperialism.*

# 14

## A NEW PHILIPPINES

### A New Economic System

As in the later years of Spanish colonial government in Manila, government revenue during the American regime came from poll taxes (formerly called the cédula personal), import and export tariffs, industrial and commercial licences, documentary stamps, monopolies, special Chinese taxes, real estate taxes, etc. Municipal income came from public markets, fisheries, butcheries, property taxes.

The Americans continued the system, but made some changes. The poll tax was reduced to only one *peseta* ($0.10). The polo, also called *prestación personal*, was removed; and instead infrastructure began to be built by paid laborers. Canceled also were monopolies, like on the sale of opium, the management of cockpits, the manufacture and sale of rum, etc.

All money collected by the government was deposited in the public treasury. It was supervised under a Bureau of Treasury, whose head was the insular treasurer.

It is, therefore, wrong to say expenses for the Philippines came from American taxpayers' money, for the Philippines was self-supporting from the beginning of the American occupation of Manila.

For long-term economic growth, however, the Americans had no plans for the Philippines in the beginning. A few were hoping that the new American colony might serve as the stepping stone to profitable trade with China.

In 1909, the Payne-Aldrich Tariff Act, and in 1913, the Underwood-Simmons Act, allowed free entry of Philippine rice, sugar, and tobacco into the U.S. market within a limited quota. The Philippines profited from this arrangement. In 1900, Philippine exports totaled about $4 million. In 1909, exports increased to $15 million. In 1912, exports rose to $47 million. After the First World War, prices went up and Philippine export revenue soared to $200 million.

At first glance, it seems there was much increase in revenue. Unfortunately, the ordinary Filipino did not share in this bonanza. Only the rich hacienda-owners enjoyed the new profits. The Philippines was an agricultural-exporting country, the source of raw materials for the United States. Hence, only those who owned large land estates produced enough products to export, while the landless Filipinos hired themselves as farmhands for a meager daily wage and remained as poor as before. Worse, there was no industrial development in the Philippines, because in exchange for the raw materials, like sugar, tobacco, abaca, and copra, the United States brought into the country their manufactured goods. This was the start of Filipino dependence on the U.S. dollar.

The free trade arrangement lulled the Filipinos into a false sense of economic prosperity. Because of the free trade arrangement, there was neither diversification nor full exploitation of the natural resources of the country. Instead, therefore, of developing as the need arose, Filipino entrepreneurs were content with merely producing and exporting enough within the free trade quota. No large-scale economic development was undertaken by the Filipinos for their own good.

The American government tried to encourage American investments in the Philippines. Two factors militated against it. First was the legal question of whether the Philippines was a foreign or an incorporated territory. If an incorporated territory, Philippine products could enter the United States tariff-free. But it was resolved that the constitution did not necessarily follow the flag, and that therefore the Philippines was foreign territory. This resolution, as just mentioned, limited free trade.

Second was the independence question. American business corporations hesitated to invest in the Philippines because they feared that once the Philippines became independent, their investments would suffer.

Before 1898, several currencies were used in the Philippines. There were the Mexican silver peso, minor copper coins, paper currency issued by several banks, such as Banco Español-Filipino (now Bank of the Philippine Islands) and the Hongkong and Shanghai Bank. To solve the confusion, the Taft government decided to inaugurate a completely new currency based on gold. On 2 March 1903, the American Congress approved the Philippine peso, equivalent to 50 American cents. Silver coins of lesser value were also minted: a silver peso, a half-peso or fifty centavos, a peseta or twenty centavos, and the *media peseta* or ten centavos. The smallest coin was one centavo or the hundredth part of the peso. Soon a five-centavo nickel coin, a copper centavo, and a half-centavo were also approved. And the legal tender in the Philippines was both the Philippine silver peso and the American gold dollar at the rate of 2 pesos to $1.

Various weights and measures were in use when the Americans came. Hemp, sugar, copra, and other products were measured by the picul, which varied between 125 and 140 pounds. The cavan, the unit for measuring corn and palay, varied as much as 10 percent. The yard also varied 10 percent, depending on whether one used the British or the Spanish. To solve this confusion, the metric system was introduced in 1906, and weights and measurements were standardized. Laws for inspection and sealing were adopted, with their corresponding sanctions.

In 1906, the Philippine Postal Savings Bank was created as a branch of the Bureau of Posts. The following year, it decreed that deposits in the Philippine Agricultural Bank (created in 1908) could earn 4–percent interest. In 1916, when the Philippine National Bank was created, the Agricultural Bank was absorbed by it.

With these savings institutions, the people gradually learned to deposit money for income-bearing purposes rather than merely hoard or keep it buried in the ground or other hiding places.

## A Pluralist Society

An important event during this period was the establishment of a schismatic church headed by Fr. Gregorio Aglipay. Born in 1860 in Batac, Ilocos Norte, the Aglipay began his studies at Letrán College and later entered the seminary in Vigan. He was ordained to the priesthood in Manila in 1889. He was then assigned as assistant priest at Indang, Cavite, where he most probably came to befriend Aguinaldo. Then he was sent to San Antonio, Nueva Ecija in 1892. In 1893, he was in Bocaue, Bulacan. In February 1896, he was transferred to San Pablo, Laguna, but he was soon moved to Victoria, Tarlac, which was only 15 kilometers from the headquarters of the revolutionary leader, General Francisco Macabulos.

On 1 May 1896, Aglipay was in Manila for an eye treatment. That same day, in Tarlac, Macabulos set up his provisional government. Between this day and 23 June, Aglipay traveled back and forth between Tarlac and Manila. The result was that on the latter date, Macabulos joined forces with Aguinaldo and recognized the latter's authority as president of an independent Philippines. Aglipay, the priest, most probably had acted as liaison.

On 5 July 1898, Aguinaldo named Aglipay commissioner, to collect funds for the revolution, as well as chief chaplain of the Philippine revolutionary forces. Because no lay person, no matter how high his civil position, could appoint to any spiritual office, these two appointments were invalid and illicit. And yet, on 21, 22, and 28 October, three manifestoes were issued with Aglipay's name justifying the new appointment and calling on all the Filipino priests to rally around Aguinaldo.

The manifestoes argued that the fall of the Spanish government in the Philippines meant the fall also of the Spanish Catholic Church. Why? Because the Spanish *Patronato real* which had linked the two institutions in a close union, no longer existed. Hence, it was the duty of the Filipino clergy to unite and take charge of the Catholic Church in the Philippines. The revolution was over, and cooperation between the Philippine government and the clergy was advisable, since it might look "odd" were the Filipino priests to remain loyal to the Spanish hierarchy. Government is always for the good of the people, the manifestoes continued, and should the priests refuse to cooperate, this would occasion suffering in the church, for which the priests would have to answer to God.

There was no significant reaction to the manifestoes, perhaps written by Mabini. There were those among the clergy who even considered their arguments fallacious. Mabini himself tried to soften the first statements by lamely announcing that the Aguinaldo government merely "recognized" Aglipay's new rank and position.

In due time, Archbishop Bernardino Nozaleda of Manila decided to take proper action against Aglipay. On 22 November 1898, the archbishop summoned the priest to explain himself. Aglipay ignored the summons, and the two others issued afterwards. On 23 January 1899, he was excommunicated. He refused to defend himself against the accusations of having exercised church authority illegitimately, openly defied legitimate church authority, issued manifestoes in his own name, and organized the clergy in a defiant move against the church. Three months later, 29 April, his excommunication was confirmed. Aglipay was no longer a Roman Catholic priest in good standing.

Up to that point, it was a matter of imposing disciplinary action against Aglipay. But it would not remain so. Around August 1899, Aglipay justified himself by issuing statements that independence from Spanish political rule was incomplete until the people were freed from the spiritual rule of the Spanish bishops. As the patriots ruled the civil government, so should the Philippine priests rule the church in the Philippines.

Some priests and lay Catholics supported Aglipay. But there would have been no formal schismatic church if no organizing genius had not channeled this religious current into an institution, a person who formulated both the doctrine and the disciplinary code necessary in any church. This organizer was Isabelo de los Reyes, Sr., imprisoned earlier by the Spanish and the American governments as an agitator.

De los Reyes was a prolific writer and a prolific father—he married three times and had twenty-eight children. His early writings *(El folklore filipino*, 2 volumes; *La época de la conquista; Historia de Filipinas)* brought him afoul of the law. On returning to the Philippines after a prison term in Barcelona, he continued writing and fighting for Philippine independence. In 1902, he organized the first Philippine labor union, the Unión Obrera Democrática (UOD), instrumental in staging labor strikes, for which he was again jailed.

On 29 June 1902, a public invitation to a meeting appeared in the newspaper, *El Grito del Pueblo*. De los Reyes claimed he had agreed to attend, provided a new Philippine church, independent and separate from the Roman Catholic Church, would be proclaimed. Because the public authorities feared it might occasion anti-American demonstrations, the meeting was banned. Nothing daunted de los Reyes who later published in the same newspaper a speech he had supposedly delivered on that occasion. When the speech appeared, the secretary of de los Reyes's own labor party, the UOD, publicly denied that de los Reyes had made such a speech; neither was the religious question discussed at the meeting. Furthermore, the people alleged by de los Reyes to have given their support for the new church (for example, Pardo de Tavera, José Alemany, José Albert, Martín Ocampo, Manuel Ortigas, and Pascual Poblete, owner of the newspaper) immediately denied any connections with the new movement. In answer, de los Reyes attacked Pardo de Tavera and Alemany in another newspaper, *El Progreso*.

But Aglipay, mentioned by de los Reyes as the first *obispo máximo* or supreme pontiff of the Philippine Independent Church, for a while kept his silence. To seek light, he made a few days' spiritual retreat and reflection at the Jesuit villa in Santa Ana. After three or four days, he left. Not much longer, in September 1902, Aglipay, now Bishop Aglipay, issued a series of "epistles" to the members of the new schismatic church, popularly known as the Aglipayan Church.

All churches need places for worship. Because many Catholic churches had been left vacant, many adherents of Aglipay forcibly occupied them. Some were handed over by their caretakers, while others were claimed by town officials who had joined the Philippine Independent Church. To protect themselves, the Catholics appealed to the government. After a number of years, the Supreme Court decided in favor of the plaintiffs and ordered the followers of Aglipay to vacate the Roman Catholic premises.

Further appeals were useless. The court ruled that even if the churches had been built by Filipinos, or paid for with tribute of Filipinos, they did not own the buildings, since carpenters who build or financiers who supply money for the construction did not necessary own what was built. More importantly, the government through the court recognized the Roman Catholic Church as a legal person, with rights of ownership which it had never relinquished.

The decision devastated the Philippine Independent Church. It showed that even if Aglipay's church was "Filipino," it was not really "the same" as the Roman Catholic Church. The court, in other words, declared that the Philippines was no longer a confessional but a pluralist state which allowed freedom of conscience. Non-Catholic Christianity and other religions would be respected.

## A New Society

It is clear that Spain and the United States changed the quality of Philippine society. Spain had christianized the disunited and unbaptized tribes, and the United States, to a considerable extent, did try to promote "peace and happiness . . . freedom . . . and self-government."

The appearance in 1900 of the first political parties in the Philippines shows the Philippines learned American democracy fast. That year, Felipe Buencamino and Hermenegildo Trinidad Pardo de Tavera formed the Federalist Party. Taft approved its aim of seeking acceptance of the Philippines as another state in the federal union of the United States of America. Established before peace had returned to the country, its immediate concern was the acceptance of American sovereignty over the Philippines, stabilization and peace, education, and autonomous government. Once the Philippines would have reasonably developed, the Federalists would petition for statehood.

The strong reaction against the Federalist program led to the formation of another political party aimed at absolute and immediate independence. At first, there were two factions, but in 1906, they coalesced into one Nationalist Party, headed by Sergio Osmeña, Sr.

Growing up politically, the Filipinos also developed culturally. New Filipino writers in English began to surface, although older authors, like Epifanio de los Santos, Claro M. Recto, Jesús M. Balmori, Manuel Bérnabe, etc. still wrote good Spanish prose and verse.

Not surprisingly, immediately after the defeat of the Spanish fleet, people had hoped for a new future as a free nation. Newspapers with meaningful titles appeared, like El Nuevo Día (The New Day), La Nueva Era (The New Era), or La Libertad (Liberty). But when the Filipinos realized that the Americans were their new masters, they also made known their feelings about it. A new publication appeared, again with the pregnant title, La Independencia (Independence).

There was a strong movement for independence and, in 1901, the American colonial government passed the Sedition Law punishing with death anyone promoting independence or separation from the United

States. This was followed a year later by the Brigandage Law, classifying as "bandits" those who engaged in guerrilla warfare against the Americans. In 1903, the Reconcentration Act relocated people to certain areas to make sure they did not join the underground antigovernment movement. And in 1907, a Flag Law forbade use of the Katipunan flag or any newly designed Philippine flag.

But in time, opposition to the American government in the Philippines disappeared completely. Salaries improved, health services multiplied, infrastructure increased. English was beginning to be widely used in the country, for people had to learn it to pass the qualification tests for positions in the government.

Because people expressed the things closest to their heart, the early decades under the American government were filled with nationalist writings. An early poet in the English language was José García Villa. An English author described his best poems as "among the most beautiful written in our time."

With broader opportunities, Filipino composers, like Nicanor Abelardo and Felipe S. Buencamino, began to create music which immediately appealed to the Filipino ear, *kundiman*s in Tagalog and Visayan. In those days before film and radio, the youth learned and sang native ditties or folk songs through the *Philippine Progressive Music Series* used in the schools. Folk dancing also became a countrywide activity. Rondallas were formed. And until the Japanese invasion, the Philippine Constabulary Band used to give public concerts every Sunday afternoon at the Luneta (today Rizal Park); in 1904, it won a prize at the St. Louis Exposition in the United States. The Philippine Symphony Orchestra was organized and certainly became the best in the Orient.

At this time, too, a sports program was started. The American game of baseball was introduced, and the Philippine national baseball team later became Asian champion. Athletic meets between the schools became a yearly feature, which included less brawny activities, such as singing, oratorical or declamation contests. In Manila, an athletic league was organized among the private schools, the predecessor of today's National Collegiate Athletic Association (NCAA) and the University Athletic Association of the Philippines (UAAP). So successful was the sports program in the Philippines that in the Berlin Olympics of 1936, Miguel White, a Bicolano, won a bronze medal for his country in the 440–meter high hurdles.

And, of course, American dress and shoe styles were imitated. The long formal dress for ladies and the tuxedo for the gentlemen were de rigueur at gala occasions. The American suit, popularly known as the *americana*, became the ordinary attire for school and office, replaced only in the 1960s by the *barong tagalog*. American cars crowded our roads, American nicknames were bandied about, and the dream of many an adventurous youth was to go see the United States. The Americanized Philippines became America's "display window of democracy in Asia."

## Suggestions for Further Reading

*(Complete information on recommended readings appears in the bibliography at the end of the book.)*

Achútegui, Pedro S. de, and Miguel A. Bernad, *Religious revolution in the Philippines;* Anderson, Gerald H., *Studies in Philippine church history;* Forbes, W. Cameron, *The Philippine Islands;* Golay, Frank H. (ed.), *Philippine-American relations;* Grunder, Garel, and William Livezey, *The Philippines and the United States;* May, Glenn Anthony, *Social engineering in the Philippines: The aims, execution, and impact of the American colonial policy, 1900–1913;* Owen, Norman G., et al., *Compadre colonialism: Philippine-American relations, 1898–1946.*

# 15

## THE DIFFICULT ROAD TO INDEPENDENCE

### Political Activities

In 1903, two years after peace had returned, the first Philippine national census was taken. Four years later, in 1907, national elections were held for the members of the lower legislative chamber, the National Assembly. The Philippine Commission, till then the only legislature, now became the upper chamber in the new bicameral Philippine legislative body.

The majority of those elected to the National Assembly, as the lower body was called, belonged to the Nationalist Party (Nacionalistas), whose platform was immediate independence for the Philippines. Only sixteen represented the opposition party, the National Progressive Party, as the old Federalist Party (Federalistas) was now called. The rest were unaffiliated or independent politicians.

For the next fifteen years, 1907–1922, the Nacionalista Party headed by Sergio Osmeña, continued as the majority party. It was clear that its program for "immediate" independence was the reason why the Nationalists continued as the majority party in the government. But it had its shortcomings, too. "Independence" served as the convenient tool for election even of unqualified candidates.

In 1914, Teodoro Sandico formed a third party, the Democrat Party (Democratas), among those who thought Osmeña was too subservient to the Americans and those who charged that the three traditional branches of government—the legislative, the executive, and the judiciary—were no longer independent or free of one another.

In 1916, the Jones Law provided that Philippine independence would be granted as soon as the Philippines had a "stable" government. A Senate, composed of elected Filipinos, replaced the Philippine Commission as the upper legislative chamber, and the House of Representatives continued as the lower body. Manuel L. Quezon was elected Senate president, while Osmeña remained as Speaker of the House of Representatives.

Filipinization of the administration advanced under the governorship of Francis B. Harrison. He believed that, in keeping with the Jones Law,

114

the Filipinos should run their own government as much as possible, preparatory to their complete independence.

In 1918, Harrison established a Council of State, to advise the governor general and facilitate cooperation between the legislature and the executive branches. It was composed of Governor Harrison himself (president), Speaker Osmeña (vice-president), Senate President Quezon, and members of the governor's cabinet.

Consulted by the governor general on all important issues, Osmeña—Speaker of the House of Representatives, head of the majority party, and vice-president of the Council of State—was the most powerful Filipino political leader in the country. Taft had already described him as the "Number Two" citizen in the Philippines after the governor. The national budget had to be approved by the Council of State before presentation to the legislature. Draft laws were decided by the Council of State before submitting them for debate in the National Assembly. And top positions in government-backed corporations were reserved for members of the Council of State and of the majority party. All of these needed Osmeña's approval. In other words, the Philippine government was strongly centralized and depended almost exclusively on the individual who headed the majority party. This was the root of "pork-barrel politics" in the Philippines.

To continue the campaign for Philippine independence, a Commission on Independence was created in 1918. Every year, except in 1920, 1921, 1929, and 1934, the commission sent an independence mission to the United States to use every legal means to free the country, lobby before the American Congress, and publicize the Philippine question. But only one mission obtained concrete results, the OSROX Mission (headed by Osmeña and Manuel Roxas) in 1931–1932, which obtained the Hare-Hawes-Cutting Law on Philippine independence.

After long debates and an interruption because of national elections, the American lower house passed the draft bill authored by Congressman Butler Hare. About eight months later, on 17 December 1932, the American Congress passed a unified Independence Law from the draft bills sponsored in the Senate by Senators Harry B. Hawes and Bronson M. Cutting, and Hare in the House of Representatives. Among the more important clauses, it provided for a transition period of ten years before absolute independence, gradual tariffs on Philippine exports to the United States, and an annual quota of only fifty Filipinos immigrants to the United States. Vetoed by President Herbert Hoover, the United States Congress overrode the presidential veto by impressive margins.

After thirty-two years under the Americans, legally and without firing a bullet, the Philippines had succeeded in winning its independence (albeit at a promised later date), the first colony in modern history to do so peacefully and with the consent of the mother country.

Unfortunately, Quezon, who had no hand in obtaining the Hare-Hawes-Cutting Law (H-H-C), used all his political savvy to prevent its acceptance in the Philippines. Publicly, opposition stemmed from four unacceptable provisions of the law: namely, the undefined powers of the American official representatives in the Philippines; the long-range negative effects of the trade relations; the immigration quota; and the military, naval, and other reservations that contradicted true independence. But some observers remarked that the real reason for its "unacceptability" was that the law had been negotiated by OSROX and not by Quezon. The latter stood to lose in his political standing before the people!

After a passionate debate, the legislature voted down the independence law and, at the same time, named a joint legislative committee headed by Quezon to work for a better independence law.

## The Philippine Commonwealth

Quezon arrived in Washington, D.C. on 7 December 1933. Although coldly received, he went about his task. He talked with several key congressmen, and finally had an interview with the president.

Two weeks later, on 15 January 1934, Quezon presented the written proposals he had been asked to submit. He suggested either independence within two or three years, with limited free trade during those two or three years, and reciprocal trade relations after independence; or independence in six years, or 1940, with autonomy in the meantime, and then special trade relations to continue after independence.

Then President Franklin D. Roosevelt suggested some kind of a compromise. Senator Millard Tydings and Representative John McDuffie of Alabama conferred with the Filipino leaders. Subsequently, Tydings and McDuffie sponsored a bill much like the H-H-C, but with the provisions for military reservations deleted. Instead, the new law provided that after independence, both countries would work for an "ultimate settlement" of American naval and refueling stations in the Philippines.

On 19 March, the House of Representatives, and on 23 March, the Senate passed the Tydings-McDuffie Law, the new independence law of the Philippines. President Roosevelt signed it on 24 March, and the Philippine legislature unanimously accepted it on 1 May 1934.

In accordance with the Tydings-McDuffie law, the Philippines would become a commonwealth for a ten-year transition period before absolute independence in 1946. Accordingly, on 30 July 1934, a constitutional convention started work on a new constitution, the fundamental law of the land. Presided over by Claro M. Recto, the convention ended on 15 February 1935. Roosevelt approved the new Philippine Constitution a month later, and on 14 May, a national plebiscite ratified it. On 17 September, national elections were held. Quezon was elected president of the commonwealth; Osmeña, vice-president. On 15 November 1935, they took their oaths of office.

During the commonwealth period, the Philippine population was estimated at about 16 million, an increase from the 1903 population of 10.3 million. This was due to better health services and better living conditions.

But the Philippines continued to be a poor country. And Filipinos themselves were mainly responsible. The preferential trade arrangement petrified the few export enterprises in the country. Instead of seeking new markets outside of the United States, or initiating other industries, they concentrated on what had been arranged under the free quota system. The sugar industry, for example, enjoying a free quota, stagnated within the limit set for it. The government corporations in charge of the rice, corn, coconut, and fiber industries were saddled with inefficiency and victimized by malversation of funds.

The economic difficulties of the Philippine Commonwealth is perhaps best illustrated in the inadequate public school system. In 1937, one-fifth of the annual budget was set aside for education. In 1941, four years later, the share of the schools was increased to more than one-third. But this was merely a 10–percent increase in the school budget, not enough to provide schooling for the 40–percent increase in student population. There were fewer and fewer classrooms, fewer books, fewer blackboards, and even fewer teachers whose salaries were the lowest of all public employees. Faced with the difficulty, the government decided to shorten the elementary school program to only six years.

In his election campaign speeches, Quezon promised he would start a social justice program as a remedy. But when he became commonwealth president, not much was done to fulfill his promise. In fact, the social problems of Central Luzon started during Quezon's presidency.

The Rice Tenancy Act, for example, was passed to regulate relations between landowners and tenants. But section 29 of this law provided that it would take effect only on approval by the town councils. Because Philippine town councils were composed of local magnates and landowners, the law remained a dead letter.

In 1936, Quezon also announced that the plan to purchase large haciendas and resell them as small plots would not be carried out. Early in the century, he explained, the Americans had already tried the same thing. They had bought the friar lands, and resold them to small landowners. But they ended up in the hands of the few rich, anyway. And Quezon said it would be risky for the commonwealth to repeat what had already failed. The landless continued without land, the few rich continued to be rich.

To improve the situation, a Joint Preparatory Committee on Philippine Affairs was established. It extended to fifteen years the period of limited free trade with the United States, but with regressive duty-free quotas instead of increasing the tariffs on Philippine exports. But the outbreak of the Second World War and the Japanese sneak attack on Pearl Harbor nullified everything.

Likewise, Quezon saw that the Philippines was militarily unprepared for independence. The Tydings-McDuffie Law included an article about Philippine neutrality, but action in that direction had not been taken. When Japan invaded Manchuria in the 1930s, and later, when Hitler invaded Poland in 1939, Quezon's worst fears were realized.

In 1936, he had already asked Douglas MacArthur, soon to retire from the U.S. Army, to act as his military adviser, with the title "Field Marshall." Asked by Quezon if he thought the Filipinos could defend themselves, MacArthur replied he did not think they could, he *knew* they could.

Defense and military preparations were duly started. Quezon himself announced that every Filipino was bound to defend and even die for his country. Because of the poor economy, Philippine military buildup would be gradual and mainly "passively defensive." But he wanted to tell future invaders of his country that

> the citizens of these islands are not to be subjugated; that the conquest of this nation cannot be accomplished short of utter destruction, and that destruction would involve such staggering cost to an aggressor, both in blood and gold, that even the boldest and strongest will unerringly mark the folly of such an undertaking.

All this time, Japan was engaged in an expansion program. In 1937, she invaded China. When France fell under Hitler's *Blitzkrieg* (or lightning war), Japanese troops occupied French Indochina (today Cambodia, Laos, and Vietnam), and from there penetrated about 600 kilometers into mainland China.

Cordell Hull, the American secretary of state, warned Japan of possible negative American public opinion. After 15 October 1940, the export of iron and steel scrap to countries outside of the western hemisphere (clearly meaning Japan) was forbidden, prompting the Japanese ambassador at Washington, D. C. to qualify the decisions as an "unfriendly act." Less than a year later, on 26 July 1941, the American government froze Japanese credits in the United States. The British did the same. Meanwhile in the Philippines, General MacArthur was named commander in chief of the United States Army Forces in the Far East (USAFFE).

## The Japanese Invasion

On 17 August, President Roosevelt had already warned that military action by Japan would force his country to take immediate steps to defend her interests. He insisted that the United States disapproved forced change of the governments of nations, and asked Japan to withdraw troops from Indochina and China and return the situation to normal.

A month later, a new government in Japan was installed. Admiral Kichisaburo Nomura and a special Japanese envoy were sent to reopen trade relations with the United States. But the Japanese government insisted that war preparations should continue in case peaceful negotiations availed nothing.

On 29 November 1941, Secretary of State Cordell Hull informed the British government that negotiations with Japan had come to a standstill. At about 3:00 A.M. of 8 December (Manila time), Japanese sea and air forces launched a surprise attack on the United States naval base in Pearl Harbor in Hawaii and, later in the day on military installations in the Philippines. Totally unprepared, the United States lost her entire Pacific defensive arm, leaving the Japanese forces an unopposed field for conquest. All the efforts of Quezon and Osmeña towards Philippine independence were neutralized by the Japanese war planes.

The story of the Japanese invasion of the Philippines was short and swift: 8 December, the Japanese bombed American planes in Manila and the other bases in Luzon; 11 December, Japanese soldiers landed in Aparri, Cagayan; 12 December, more planes destroyed Nichols Field and the Cavite Navy Yard; 13 December, Japanese troops occupied Legazpi, Albay; 14 December, they were in Damortis, La Union; 20 December, Davao fell; 22 December, Lt. Gen. Masaharu Homma landed with a major Japanese force at Lingayen, Pangasinan. To effect a junction with them, another large contingent landed in Atimonon, Tayabas (now Quezon). And so, Japanese troops advancing unopposed towards Manila doomed the city.

On 24 December, MacArthur ordered the commonwealth officials and their families to Corregidor Island. Before leaving, Quezon instructed Secretary of Justice José P. Laurel and Presidential Secretary Jorge B. Vargas to cooperate with the Japanese short of taking the oath of allegiance to the Japanese imperial government. On 26 December, Manila was declared an open city, in the hope of saving it from further bombing. Finally, on the last day of 1941, MacArthur regrouped the retreating Filipino and American troops in Bataan, where he planned to stay on until American reenforcements arrived.

In the United States, a strategic decision was announced. Allied defenses would concentrate on the European front first before initiating the Pacific counteroffensive. It was, therefore, only a matter of time before the ill-fed, undermanned, and inadequately armed soldiers in Bataan would fall before the Japanese invaders. And although the gallant stand by the Philippine and American forces in Bataan and Corregidor— the scene of the last efforts to repel the invaders—delayed the Japanese war timetable, they finally succumbed to the reenforced strength of the Japanese. On 9 April 1942, after a last desperate effort in the face of inhuman difficulties, the exhausted defenders of Bataan surrendered. Field commander Gen. Edward P. King accepted the Japanese terms, and the American Stars and Stripes, together with the Filipino Sun and Stars, was hauled down. In their place, the Rising Sun of the Japanese flag was raised. But the defeated forces in Bataan accomplished one thing: at least, they stopped for a while the Japanese war machine, and saved Australia from actual invasion.

Instead of surrendering to the Japanese, however, many of the troops escaped to Corregidor. But those who gave themselves up were forced to hike under the scorching April sun from Mariveles, Bataan to San Fernando, Pampanga. In this "death march," the Japanese shot or bayoneted anyone who attempted to deviate from the line of march, or even lingered to take a drink or rest. In San Fernando, they herded the captives into a train which took them north to a concentration camp in Capas, Tarlac. In a barracks built for 20,000, 60,000 war prisoners were crowded. Hungry, exhausted, ill-clothed, ill-fed, and sick, men died by the thousands. Some estimate that around 45,000 died in the camp, besides the 25,000 who had already fallen during the forced march.

The last chapter of this tragic story of valor was set in Corregidor Island. Lt. Gen. Jonathan Wainwright commanded 11,000 troops to oppose 25,000, supported by air, navy, and land attack. Fighting was fierce, but Wainwright saw the futility of further resistance. On 6 May 1942, he signed an unconditional surrender to the Japanese. Many wept when they saw the Philippine flag being brought down as the red and white Japanese flag was raised. The Philippines, again, was under a new master.

Government in the Philippines was immediately placed in the hands of an Executive Commission, a group of Filipino officials closely supervised by the Japanese Military Administration. But the Filipinos continued to defy, at least secretly, the invaders. Several joined the underground resistance movement. And although the country had a civilian (José P. Laurel) as titular head of the Japanese-sponsored government, it was virtually under martial law. Curfew hours were imposed, radios were banned unless tuned in to Japanese propaganda, private cars were impounded, etc. Continuing war conditions and the shortage of food occasioned inflation; and the Japanese occupation currency which was being circulated (facetiously dubbed "Mickey Mouse" money) could buy practically nothing.

To counteract the American promise of independence in 1946, the Japanese "granted" it earlier to the Philippines. A Preparatory Commission for Philippine Independence headed by Laurel was created and drafted a constitution. Finished on 4 September 1943, the new constitution was ratified three days later. On the 20th, delegates to the National Assembly, as provided for in the constitution, were elected. On the 23rd, the Assembly was inaugurated, and it proceeded to elect Laurel as president of the Philippines. Finally, on 14 October 1943, solemn ceremonies inaugurated the Japanese-sponsored Republic of the Philippines.

Efforts at legitimacy were not spared to approximate a peacetime government. The Executive Committee was abolished and new executive bureaus and departments were created. The judiciary was also reformed, a Foreign Office was set up with corresponding consulates in countries the Japanese had conquered.

But the Japanese failed to win the people over. Perhaps it was because traditional democratic freedoms had been curtailed: newspapers were censored, and school texts were edited to delete any reference to American or British culture.

To further Japanese aims in the country, street names were changed, and the Japanese language, Nippongo, was taught. The Kapisanan sa Paglilingkod sa Bagong Pilipinas (KALIBAPI) was also organized. Unfortunately in "promoting" Japanese rule, its members, abetted by the Japanese military, did not stop short of physical torture. By and large, too, the Japanese soldiers abused the people, beating them harshly for no apparent reason. Hungry from fighting at the front, they robbed the people of their food, their jewelry, and even of their clothes. When a guerrilla or an underground unit killed a lone Japanese sentry, entire villages were made to pay for the deed. The Japanese would round up the men of the village in a house which they then set on fire, and they would shoot or bayonet those who tried to escape.

There was another angle to the story. Just as there were underground resistance or guerrilla fighters, there were also those who openly or secretly collaborated with the Japanese. The guerrillas lived in the hills, sniped at Japanese detachments, destroyed lines of communication, spied on Japanese movements, and relayed information to the Allied headquarters. Their activities helped prepare for the counteroffensive and would be instrumental in the success of MacArthur's campaign.

On the other hand, among the collaborators who aided the enemy, there were those who joined the infamous Makabayang Katipunan ng mg Pilipino (MAKAPILI), an organization whose aim was for members to spy and tell on their fellow Filipinos. And then there were others, perhaps out of fear or in the belief that the Allied forces had abandoned the Philippines for good, acted as informers for the Japanese. There were also quite a number of "war barons." They became rich by buying war materials from private persons and reselling them for a handsome profit to the Japanese.

## Suggestions for Further Reading

*(Complete information on recommended readings appears in the bibliography at the end of the book.)*

Churchill, Bernardita R., *The Philippine independence missions to the United States, 1919–1934;* Friend, Theodore, *Between two empires: The ordeal of the Philippines, 1929–1946;* Hayden, Joseph R., *The Philippines: A study in national development;* Kalaw, Máximo, *The development of Philippine politics, 1872–1920;* Liang, Dapen, *Philippine political parties and politics.*

# 16

## INDEPENDENT PHILIPPINES

### Liberation

Before Corregidor fell to the Japanese, General MacArthur escaped to Australia on orders of President Franklin D. Roosevelt. On his arrival there, he made his famous pledge, "I have come through and I shall return." Two-and-a-half years later, on 20 October 1944, he would redeem his pledge. From Tacloban, Leyte, the first city to be liberated by the American forces from Japan, he would voice over the radio his equally famous words, "People of the Philippines, I have returned."

The MacArthur-led Allied counteroffensive was, like the earlier Japanese advance, unstoppable. Starting on 9 August 1944, American bombers hit Davao. On 12 August, they bombed the Visayan Islands. On 21 September, Japanese shipping facilities in Manila were destroyed. On 20 October, the first American landing was secured on Leyte beach near Tacloban. MacArthur, followed by Osmeña, the commonwealth president after Quezon died in Lake Saranac, New York on 1 August, waded ashore. Next, the Americans conquered Mindoro and made it a base of operations. It was more convenient to operate from Mindoro than from Leyte because Mindoro was on the western side and therefore affected by fewer typhoons.

Successful guerrilla activity had been intense. Their underground network of spies and radio communications had proved invaluable, and their diversionary tactics drew Japanese defenses to Southern Luzon. MacArthur landed unopposed in Lingayen, Pangasinan on 9 January 1945. Another force landed in Nasugbu, Batangas on 31 January, while paratroopers jumped down on Tagaytay three days later. That same day, armed tanks and jeeps of the American First Cavalry Division rumbled from the north into Manila through Balintawak and Rizal Avenue.

Fighting was fiercest in Manila itself. The Japanese retreated into Intramuros and barricaded themselves behind the walls of the buildings and houses on its narrow streets. In desperation, they went into a frenzy of killing, victimizing innocent noncombatants, Filipinos and foreigners, men, women, and children.

But the end was near. On 23 February 1945, with the whole city almost totally razed to the ground—an American inspection team thought Manila was the second most devastated city after Warsaw during the Second World War—organized Japanese resistance ended. MacArthur's forces moved elsewhere: North Luzon, Central Visayas, Central Luzon, Southern Luzon—all surrendered to the mightier weaponry of the American liberators. On 5 July 1945, the Philippines was liberated from the Japanese.

But the final outcome of the war is only indirectly part of Philippine history, for it was decided elsewhere. After refusing an ultimatum to surrender, Japan saw two of its big cities wiped out by the first atomic bombs ever used in war: Hiroshima on 6 August, and Nagasaki three days later. Finally, on 2 September 1945, aboard the USS *Missouri*, the Japanese command signed unconditional terms of surrender to the Allies.

The nightmare of war had finally ended, and the Philippines awoke to a new reality. President Osmeña faced the mammoth job of rebuilding a nation almost totally destroyed by war. And the first major tasks to be taken up were the normalization of government, the healing of a devastated economy, and the settling of the collaboration issue.

On 27 February 1945, MacArthur turned over Malacañan Palace to Osmeña. But residence in the governor's palace did not help much in easing the problems of the new commonwealth president. MacArthur's primary objective had been to defeat Japan and as he advanced northward, he had left Osmeña with hardly any resources to rebuild the devastated nation. With the war over, he now admitted he could not, because of personality differences, work with Osmeña. Moreover, he thought Roxas, suspected of having collaborated with the Japanese, was the better man to lead the country. To catapult his choice legitimately to the highest office of the Philippines, MacArthur exonerated Roxas of all charges against him, and pressured Osmeña to hold presidential elections.

At a time when the Filipinos needed food and other material help to recover from the destruction of war, MacArthur forced them to play the political game of presidential elections. And so, while Osmeña was in the United States soliciting aid for his country, Roxas was electioneering. Not only that; probably with MacArthur's consent, the latter used U. S. Army equipment, like radios, transportation, etc., to further his presidential campaign.

Osmeña had no chance against Roxas's well-organized campaign machinery. Furthermore, he was preoccupied with settling the key political issue of the independence of the Philippines. Would it be granted on the original date stipulated in the Tydings-McDuffie Law?

Would it perhaps be better to postpone the date until the nation would have recovered from the war?

Osmeña was also troubled by the fact that—despite the publicized promise made by President Roosevelt at the start of the Japanese war to return to the Filipinos everything "to the last carabao and hut"—Harry S. Truman, Roosevelt's successor, told Osmeña that help for the rehabilitation of the Philippines would come only if the collaboration issue was settled.

And so, besides having to campaign for his election, Osmeña had to confront a multiplicity of problems.

Not surprisingly, Roxas won the election. On 28 May 1946, he took his oath of office as the third president of the Philippine Commonwealth. He was the last of the line, for on 4 July, a little less than two months later, the Philippines was declared a sovereign and independent republic. Manuel Roxas automatically became the first president of the new republic.

## Problems of Independence

Although seemingly simple, the question of the Japanese collaborators turned out to be a complicated issue. The American Military Command wanted to penalize all collaborators; but MacArthur believed they fell under the jurisdiction of the Philippine, not the American, government, and left Osmeña to settle the issue. But, had the war been against the Philippines, or against the United States? The Philippines was indeed an American colony, but were the Filipinos obliged to keep allegiance to the United States after it had failed to protect them from the Japanese?

To the Americans, anyone who had sided with the enemy was a collaborator. In Roosevelt's phrase, those who had "collaborated with the enemy must be removed from authority and influence in the political and economic life of the country."

Osmeña thought suspects should be judged not just *by* their *actions*, but by their *reasons* for their actions. He had made it clear his government was going to be one of law, and "not the mere act of occupying office under the Japanese but *the motive in doing so and the record in office* would be the measure of one's loyalty."

During the Japanese occupation, there were Filipinos who were coerced into working with the Japanese. For example, teachers, mail carriers, bus drivers, etc. who had to earn a salary, and whose services were needed to allow life to continue as normally as possible. Others, especially the political leaders, had to cooperate with the invaders to save the rest of the nation from unnecessary vexation and suffering. A third group was comprised of those who were clearly anti-American and pro-Japanese from the beginning. Of these three, then, who collaborated traitorously with the Japanese?

There were, then, no clear norms for judging. In June 1945, a People's Court was opened to try collaboration cases. But there were too many for too few trial judges. For an estimated 5,600 cases, there were only fifteen authorized judges. The country was divided into five judicial districts, and twenty-five government prosecutors were allowed only six months to present their case. This meant an average of 315 cases every day, including Sunday. This was clearly an impossible task.

Roxas inherited the unresolved collaboration issue from the previous presidency. But after the war, unity and cooperation were needed to rebuild the nation, not accusations and counteraccusations. On January 1948, he issued his Amnesty Proclamation for all. The suspects, it said, had either been forced to cooperate with the Japanese, or clearly considered it a patriotic thing to do. Finally, the act declared, "all the Filipinos favored" amnesty in order to put it behind them and start the more important task of rehabilitating the country, for the more serious problem was the economic devastation of the Philippines. Like Osmeña, Roxas sought American economic aid. The United States' answer came in the form of the Philippine Trade Act and the Philippine Rehabilitation Act of 1946.

The first provided for free trade for eight years, after which tariffs would gradually increase until 1974, when full tariffs would be imposed on Philippine exports to the United States. The Philippine peso was tied to the American dollar (2 pesos = $1), and American citizens received equal or parity rights with the Filipinos in the "disposition, exploitation, development and utilization of all agricultural, timber, and mineral lands of the public domain, the waters, minerals, coal, petroleum, and mineral resources of the Philippines, and the operation of public utilities."

Because the Philippine Constitution provided that only corporations in which at least 60 percent of the capital was owned by Filipinos could so operate, the constitution had to be amended in order to receive aid from the same nation for whose sake the Philippines had been victimized by a war! But changes in the fundamental law of the land needed to be approved by a majority vote of three-fourths in the legislature before being ratified in a national plebiscite. To obtain this majority, the Roxas government refused to seat seven representatives-elect from Central Luzon and three senators-elect who were known opponents of the parity clause, on the pretext that they had been elected through fraud and terrorism. Parity then won in the Philippine Congress—but by only one vote! Appealed to the Supreme Court, the high tribunal later declared that if the votes of the ousted members "had been counted, the affirmative votes [for parity] would have been short of the necessary three-fourths vote."

This political maneuver to obtain economic help from a country for whose sake the Philippines had been destroyed, broke the faith of the people of Central Luzon in the government. The social problem in Central Luzon turned into a serious military problem, giving rise to the HUKBALAHAP insurgency. The Philippine economy became tied to the American dollar. American manufactured goods flooded the country, and the Philippines continued to be the source of raw materials for the United States.

The Rehabilitation Act gave the Philippines the following: $620 million as compensation for damages sustained during the war; $100 million in the form of surplus or second-hand American equipment and machinery; $120 million to restore damaged public property and utilities; $400 million for individual claimants and corporations who could prove they had suffered from the war.

This double aid was not the best, of course, but it was urgently needed by the country. Before aid was released, the Philippines had to swallow some humiliating conditions, like the parity clause just mentioned, or the amendment of the Philippine Constitution in order to have claims exceeding the small amount of $500 acknowledged by the Unites States. As Congressman Bell chortled, the rehabilitation bill assured the United States of "our sixth best customer in world commerce." An independent Philippines remained economically chained to the United States.

## The Philippine Left

Perhaps the social problem that erupted in Central Luzon best illustrates the sad state of the Philippines during the first years of independence. It was a social problem that had been fermenting for decades, and catalyzed by the rise of the Philippine left.

In May 1930, a convention was held by the Philippine Labor Congress, a labor organization headed by Crisanto Evangelista, who had been trained in Moscow. It was a stormy meeting and, at the end, a group seceded, calling itself Katipunan ng mga Anakpawis sa Pilipinas (Philippine Association of the Children of Sweat) or KAP. About three months later, on 20 August, KAP formally adopted the communist ideology and practical program.

Soon after, it staged a number of demonstrations and labor strikes. It also started its own newspaper, *Titis* (Spark). But two years later, the government outlawed the organization.

In 1932, Pedro Abad Santos formed another labor party, the Socialist Party of the Philippines or SPP. When the American communist James S. Allen, also known as Dr. Sol Auerbach, suggested that the communists in the Philippines merge with other groups to fight Mussolini's expanding fascism, Abad Santos agreed. This merger in 1938 between the KAP and SPP became the first Communist Party of the Philippines (CPP).

When the Pacific War broke out in December 1941, the CPP had already organized the Hukbo ng Bayan Laban sa Hapon (National Anti-Japanese Army) or HUKBALAHAP. Its alleged aim was to fight the Japanese, but it was actually the CPP military arm.

The Huks suffered a serious loss of leaders during the Japanese war. Some were killed by the Japanese secret police, or KEMPETAI; others were arrested and kept in jail.

Yet the Huks did creditably well during the war. They harassed the enemy continually, killed them whenever they could, and seized the arms of the dead. They engaged the Japanese in an estimated 1,200 skirmishes and battles, killed about 25,000 Japanese soldiers and Filipino puppets. When MacArthur returned to liberate the Philippines, their numbers had reached about 20,000 fully armed regulars and 50,000 reservists.

After the war, several Huk followers and communists stayed in Manila. They were still an underground society, since communism had been outlawed in 1932. But in 1949, inspired by the successful campaign of the Chinese communists, they decided to come out into the open.

As mentioned, the occasion was the ouster in 1946 of six congressmen-elect from Central Luzon: Luis Taruc and Amado Yuzon (Pampanga), Jesús Lava (Bulacan), José Cando and Constancio Padilla (Nueva Ecija), and Alejandro Simpauco (Tarlac).

Manuel Roxas had tried the iron hand, but failed to defeat the growing menace of communist insurgency. He died suddenly on 15 April 1948, and Vice-President Elpidio Quirino succeeded him. Later, in 1950, Quirino was elected president in his own right. Perhaps his most far-reaching appointment was that of Ramón Magsaysay, congressman from Zambales whom he named secretary of national defense. Magsaysay broke the Huk movement.

This is how it happened, according to Alfredo B. Saulo, once a member of the Huks:

The first thing that Magsaysay did as defense chief was to cleanse the AFP [Armed Forces of the Philippines] of undesirable elements in order to regain the faith and confidence of the people. An experienced guerrilla fighter, Magsaysay himself led government forces in many difficult operations against the Huks. But, as it happened, the greatest achievement of Magsaysay as an anti-communist fighter was not planned but came by accident.

Tarcisio Rizal, alias Arthur, a grandson of the national hero and a disenchanted Huk commander, approached Magsaysay one day in September 1950 and gave him vital information on the whereabouts of the CPP hierarchy in Manila. . . . Early in the morning of 18 October, twenty-two AFP intelligence teams, assisted by Manila policemen, swooped down on communist hideouts in the city. Among those arrested were Jose Lava (alias Harry, Felix Cruz, Gaston); Federico Maclang (Eto, O. Beria, Olivas, Mariano Cruz); Ramon Espiritu (Johnny); Iluminada Calonge (Luming); Angel Baking; and Sammy Rodriguez.

The communists had been poised to strike and take over the government of the Philippines. But the capture of their leaders, documents, weapons, and funds severely crippled the organization. The communist movement had never enjoyed the support of the majority of the Filipinos, and it has stayed underground, surfacing only to attack and ambush their enemies as well as innocent victims.

Superficially, the claim of the communists that they were fighting for justice could win over the unwary. Their objectives were both "short-range" and "long-range." The first include the following:

1. Expropriation of large estates for redistribution to the landless
2. Job opportunities by Filipinizing industry
3. Decent wages and salary increases to employees
4. Low-cost housing
5. Nationalization of basic industries, e.g., iron, banking, transportation, communication, rice, corn, etc.
6. Establishment of cooperatives and rural credit agencies
7. Free, compulsory education till high school
8. Sufficient clinics and hospitals for the poor
9. Promotion and development of Philippine culture
10. Trade relations and diplomatic ties with all countries
11. Revocation of the parity-clause amendment of the constitution
12. Withdrawal of American military bases from the Philippines

There is no quarrel with these aims. They are the same objectives of any welfare or socialist state. The problem is their final program, their long-range policy. They would not be communists if they did not seek the overthrow of the democratic government of the Philippines. In traditional Leninist style, they do not care about the means, for any method will do, even immoral. The most attractive appeal is their claim to be "nationalists."

However, the recent disintegration of communism in Russia and the Russian satellites in Eastern Europe has unmasked the pretenses of the Marxist-Leninist dream of so-called justice and equality for all.

## Suggestions for Further Reading

*(Complete information on recommended readings appears in the bibliography at the end of the book.)*

Abaya, Hernando J., *Betrayal in the Philippines;* Abaya, Hernando, J., *The untold Philippine story;* Abueva, José V., *Ramón Magsaysay: A political biography;* Agoncillo, Teodoro A., *The burden of proof: The Vargas-Laurel collaboration case;* Economic Survey Mission to the Philippines, *Report to the president of the United States;* Kerkvliet, Benedict, *The Huk rebellion: A study of peasant revolt in the Philippines;* Lachica, Eduardo, *Huk: Philippine agrarian society in revolt;* Lichauco, Marcial P., *Roxas: The story of a great Filipino and of the political era in which he lived;* Malay, Armando J., *Occupied Philippines: The role of Jorge B. Vargas during the Japanese occupation;* Pomeroy, William J., *American neo-colonialism: Its emergence in the Philippines and Asia;* Pomeroy, William J., *The forest;* Saulo, Alfredo B., *Communism in the Philippines: An introduction;* Shalom, Stephen R., "Philippine acceptance of the Bell Trade Act of 1946," *PHR* 49; Smith, Robert Aura, *Philippine freedom, 1946–1958;* Taruc, Luis, *He who rides the tiger.*

# 17

# A YOUNG REPUBLIC

## Prospects for Growth

Before the 1986 EDSA Revolution, seven presidents had governed the Philippines since independence in 1946: Manuel Roxas, 1946–1948; Elpidio Quirino, 1948–1954; Ramón Magsaysay, 1954–1957; Carlos P. García, 1957–1962; Diosdado Macapagal, 1962–1966; Ferdinand E. Marcos, 1966–1986.

Except for Marcos who twisted the constitution to perpetuate himself in power, no one was ever reelected. Two, Roxas and Magsaysay, died in office. As a result, there was no continuity of presidential policies, for every four years a new president assumed the national leadership. He might introduce his own special programs during his term, but the succeeding president, always from the rival political party, laid them aside and drafted his own.

During Roxas's term, as mentioned, the government tried force to defeat communism. It failed. However, two pieces of legislation were approved: the Tenancy Act, which provided a 70–percent share of profits for the landlord and 30–percent for the tenant; and the charter which established the Central Bank of the Philippines.

After Liberation, people, in reaction to years of deprivation, had a fit of spending for items they had missed during the war. The few dollars available in the country were dissipated in luxury items, like nylon stockings and lipstick for the ladies.

During Quirino's term, the Huks, inspired by the victorious Maoist Chinese, shifted from a parliamentary to a military struggle. As mentioned, Magsaysay neutralized their efforts.

However, the economy continued to be precarious. Government policies were ineffectual because private business succeeded in going around official regulations. Perhaps the best example was the government's feeble attempt to control imports. To minimize the outflow of Philippine dollar reserves, the government directed that one had to obtain a license to exchange pesos into dollars with which to import goods. What resulted? An underground peso-dollar exchange. Some "businessmen" even put up "dummy" plants and factories to show the need for dollars to get the license. And for every government economic expert, there were 100 private businessmen trying to sabotage his policies.

A shift in emphasis was made and the government encouraged exports through the production of agricultural goods, and the development of the logging industry. For a moment, exports and dollar earnings increased. But the private sector never organized itself into a force to prevent corrupt politicians from raising funds, both legally and illegally, to spend during their election campaigns.

Ramón Magsaysay proved to be the bright light in this gloomy postwar period. He proclaimed and then proved himself to be, after his election, a "president for the people." For example, for the first time, ordinary Filipinos were welcome to visit Malacañan Palace, the president's official residence. He said that a democratic government should "satisfy the needs of the common man . . . freedom from fear and freedom from want." His most famous utterance was "He who has less in life should have more in law."

Then on 17 March 1957, flying back from Cebu to Manila, his plane crashed against a mountain. The lighting system of the plane had malfunctioned and the pilot had no clear perception of depth. His craft flew straight against the mountainside and all died except one, Nestor Mata, newspaper reporter thrown out on impact.

The unprecedented numbers that lined up to pay their last respects to their dead president and accompany the funeral cortege to his final resting place was eloquent testimony of the pain that gripped the entire nation. They had seen what good government was, but, like an enjoyable dream, it quickly ended and the Filipinos woke up to harsh reality.

Vice-President Carlos P. García automatically took office as president for the remaining years of Magsaysay's term, and subsequently won election to the presidency on his merits in 1958. He was, however, not another Magsaysay. His political rivals mercilessly attacked him in the press, describing him, with some exaggeration, as "ignorant, venal, and inefficient." But graft in high and low government office reared its ugly head once again. Take this case, as reported by an American journalist: García had promised, even before the treaty was signed, to share with his supporters the Japanese war reparations fund of $300 million in the form of ships and industrial machinery. And in an effort to conserve the dwindling foreign reserves of the country, President García decreed that exporters should obtain import licenses before they could exchange their Philippine pesos to dollars. The licenses quickly became a source of illegal wealth. It was alleged that, among others, the first lady and the presidential private secretary had enriched themselves by allocating licenses in exchange for substantial financial gifts. The president was said to have earned an estimated $700 million, most of which supported García's party candidates.

What about the economy? Politicians seemed unaware or did not care to know they were leading the nation to economic ruin. Instead of bringing in goods, those who had import licenses obtained U.S. dollars and traded them in the black market at twice the legal exchange rate. With new licenses, they repeated the deal and gained immense fortunes simply by dealing in currency. As for infrastructure and industrial machinery, no one cared about these.

García's successor was Diosdado Macapagal, who in turn was succeeded by Ferdinand Marcos. Macapagal is still with us, and the memory of Marcos's presidency is still too fresh and perhaps painful to many Filipinos. We have to wait a little while longer and allow time to give us the proper perspective before we can make an objective assessment of their accomplishments as presidents of the Philippines.

### Contemporary Problems

In 1968, the Philippine population reached 36 million. In 1990, forty-four years after independence, the estimated population had grown to 63 million. Of these, 83 percent claim to be Roman Catholics, the rest are members of non-Catholic but Christian churches, like the Lutheran, the Philippine Independent Church, the Methodist, etc. Less than 5 percent are Muslims. In other words, culture is strongly Christian and human values have not yet been completely forgotten.

In 1968, too, the Greater Manila area had a population of 2.5 million. In 1990, the official estimate was 4.5 million. But this increased number includes squatter families who have migrated from the provinces in search of a livelihood, some of them forced to squat in cardboard lean-tos under bridges, sidewalks, or any unoccupied site. City streets have become too narrow for the number of cars used, schools getting too small for the burgeoning student population, business too slow for the rapidly expanding labor force.

Mere numerical growth can mislead. For example, in 1948, 7 out of every 200 houses in rural Philippines were *barong-barong* shacks, or hovels made of salvaged materials. But in 1960, the proportion worsened to 19 out of every 200 houses. In 1967, the average monthly income of the Filipinos was 55 pesos, while 31 out of every 300 adults were unemployed, or working less than eight hours daily. To supplement their income, many engaged in petty retail business, vending cigarettes, newspapers, flower garlands, lottery tickets, etc. In 1990, Filipinos continued to face very much the same problems.

For the Philippines has remained a poor country. Although the Philippines ranks high among nations in the proportion of citizens going to college or who have obtained at least the bachelor's degree, the situation is problematic. Many well-trained college graduates migrate to foreign countries where they can earn better salaries, because in the Philippines they do not earn enough to support a family. On the other hand, a not insignificant proportion of earnings in the country comes from money sent by contract workers abroad. And the existence of fake diploma syndicates who provide forged diplomas for those who wish to "qualify" for a better-paying job in the country or elsewhere, is a clear symptom of a deep malaise in the Philippine socioeconomic situation.

One serious effect of this dehumanizing poverty is the peculiar Filipino joke, "Politics is good business." An ambitious candidate is willing to spend millions during the electoral campaigns in the hope that, after election, he can have a hefty share of the profit (legal or otherwise) of being in government.

For a democracy to succeed, the electoral process should be sacred. But in the few years the secret ballot has been used by the Filipinos, the people continue to wonder whether those who govern were those who were elected. Vote buying, flying voters, terrorism, dishonest tallies have always made a mockery of Philippine elections. Not only that; many people, not yet fully aware of their rights, have yet to realize that government *begins* after the elections. People have yet to be educated in their responsibilities, that democracy is indeed government *for* the people if it is *by* the people. To succeed, Philippine democracy needs intelligent cooperation from its citizens.

## Pledge for the Future

Philippine history is unique. The Philippines was forged together by the Spanish missionaries, and Spanish Catholicism has remained its strongest influence, balanced by the North American secularistic republicanism. There have been few wars in the country, and damage to infrastructure has been due mainly to natural calamities, like typhoons, earthquakes, volcanic eruptions, fires, and floods. Although Filipinos have fought fiercely and many have shed their blood—it has often been in defense of what they believed to be just. Aggression has not characterized the Philippine past. And because Philippine independence was won through peaceful legal means, the Filipinos have committed their lives and their country's future, as Rizal dreamed, to constitutional processes.

It is not by accident that the first scholars of the country were brilliant legal minds and politicians who could compare with the best of the world. And just as Rizal was the first Asian nationalist, so also the Philippines was the first Asian colony to achieve independent status. A Filipino delegate was also one of the original signatories to the UN charter in 1945. Through Carlos P. Romulo, the Philippines pledged to uphold the dignity and equality of all human beings, their right to lead a free life, to choose one's religion. This was not an empty promise. It was a deeply held belief born of the experience that has made the Philippines a nation.

Will this pledge continue to inspire future generations?

A half century after 4 July 1946 and nearly a century after 12 June 1898, the Philippines is still a young nation. But the new republic is slowly making its own contribution to the shaping of a more just and more human world.

### Suggestions for Further Reading

*(Complete information on recommended readings appears in the bibliography at the end of the book.)*

Buss, Claude A., *The United States and the Philippines: Background for policy;* Golay, Frank H., *Philippine-American relations;* Karnow, Stanley, *In our image: America's empire in the Philippines;* Reynolds, Quentin, and Geoffrey Bocca, *Macapagal, the incorruptible;* Taylor, George E., *The Philippines and the United States: Problems of partnership.*

# BIBLIOGRAPHY

BR    Blair, Emma H., and James A. Robertson, eds. 1903–09. *The Philippine Islands, 1493–1898.* 55 vols. Cleveland: Arthur H. Clark.

PS    *Philippine Studies.* Quarterly published by the Ateneo de Manila University Press (Quezon City).

PHR   *Pacific Historical Review.* Periodical published by the Pacific Coast Branch of the American Historical Association and the University of California Press (Berkeley, Los Angeles, and London).

Abaya, Hernando J. 1946. *Betrayal in the Philippines.* New York: A.A. Wyn.

_____. 1967. *The untold Philippine story.* 3d ed. Quezon City: Malaya Books.

Abueva, José V. 1971. *Ramón Magsaysay: A political biography.* Manila: Solidaridad.

Achútegui, Pedro S. de, and Miguel A. Bernad. 1960–72. *Religious revolution in the Philippines.* 4 vols. Manila: Ateneo de Manila.

Aduarte, Diego. 1903–09. History of the Dominican province of the holy rosary. In *BR* 30:115–321, 31:23–300, 32:19–296.

Agoncillo, Teodoro A. 1956. *The revolt of the masses: The story of Bonifacio and the Katipunan.* Quezon City: University of the Philippines.

_____. 1984. *The burden of proof: The Vargas-Laurel collaboration case.* Manila: University of the Philippines Press for the U.P.–Jorge B. Vargas Filipiniana Research Center.

Aguinaldo, Emilio. 1967. *Memoirs of the revolution.* Trans. L. Colendrino-Bucu. Manila.

_____. 1969. True account of the revolution. In *Aguinaldo in retrospect,* ed. M. García. Manila: Philippine Historical Commission.

Anderson, Gerald H., ed. 1969. *Studies in Philippine church history.* Ithaca, N.Y.: Cornell University Press.

Arcilla, José S. 1970. Documents concerning the Calamba deportations of 1891. *PS* 18:577–633.

_____. 1971. The exile of a liberal in 1870, or Father Arnedo's case. *PS* 19:373–419.

_____. 1983. Christian missions to China and the Philippines. *PS* 31:468–76.

_____. 1983. The Escuela Pía, forerunner of Ateneo de Manila. *PS* 31:58–74.

_____. 1984. Ateneo de Manila: Problems and policies, 1859–1939. *PS* 32:377–98.

_____. 1988. *Understanding the Noli: Its historical context and literary influences.* Quezon City: Phoenix.

The Augustinian Recollects in the Philippines. 1903–09. In *BR* 28:300–348.

Bain, David H. 1984. *Sitting in darkness: Americans in the Philippines.* Boston: Houghton Mifflin.

Bauzon, Leslie E. 1981. *Deficit government: Mexico and the Philippine situado, 1606–1804.* Tokyo: Centre for East Asian Cultural Studies.

Bernad, Miguel A. 1972. *The Christianization of the Philippines: Problems and perspectives.* Manila: Filipiniana Book Guild.

_____. 1986. *Rizal and Spain: An essay in biographical context.* Manila: National Book Store.

Blair, Emma H., and James A. Robertson, eds. 1903–09. *The Philippine Islands, 1493–1898.* 55 vols. Cleveland: Arthur H. Clark.

Buss, Claude A. 1977. *The United States and the Philippines: Background for policy.* Washington, D.C.: American Enterprise Institute for Public Policy Research.

Chirino, Pedro. 1903–09. Relation of the Philippines Islands. In *BR* 12:169–321, 13:27–217.

Churchill, Bernardita R. 1983. *The Philippine independence missions to the United States, 1919–1934.* Manila: National Historical Institute.

Colin, Francisco. 1903–09. Jesuit missions in 1656. In *BR* 28:78–103.

Comyn, Tomás de. 1969. *State of the Philippines in 1810.* Manila: Filipiniana Book Guild.

Cushner, Nicholas P. 1971. *Spain in the Philippines.* Quezon City: Institute of Philippine Culture.

Cushner, Nicholas P., and John N. Schumacher. 1969. Burgos and the Cavite Mutiny. *PS* 17:457–529.

De Jesús, Edilberto, Jr. 1966. Aguinaldo and the Americans. *Philippine Historical Review* 1:125–67.

_____. 1981. *Tobacco monopoly in the Philippines: Bureaucratic enterprise and social change, 1766–1880.* Quezon City: Ateneo de Manila University Press.

De la Costa, Horacio V. 1953. The legal basis of Spanish imperial sovereignty. *PS* 1:155–62.

_____. 1967. Patronato real and recurso de fuerza. In *Asia and the Philippines,* 39–48. Manila: Solidaridad.

De la Costa, Horacio V., and John N. Schumacher. 1979. *The Filipino clergy: Historical studies and future perspectives.* Quezon City: Ateneo de Manila University.

Díaz-Trechuelo, María Lourdes. 1963–66. The economic development of the Philippines in the second half of the eighteenth century. *PS* 11:195–223; 12:203–31; 13:763–800; 14:65–126, 253–29.

_____. 1969. The economic background. In *The Chinese in the Philippines*, ed. A. Félix, Jr., vol. 2, 18–44. Manila: Solidaridad.

Early Franciscan missions. 1903–09. In *BR* 35:278–322.

Economic Survey Mission to the Philippines. 1950. *Report to the president of the United States.* Washington, D.C.

Félix, Alfonso, Jr., ed. 1966–69. *The Chinese in the Philippines.* 2 vols. Manila: Solidaridad.

Fenner, Bruce L. 1985. *Cebu under the Spanish flag, 1521–1896: An economic–social history.* Cebu City: San Carlos.

Filipiniana Book Guild. 1969. *Travel Accounts of the Islands, 1513–1787.* Manila.

Forbes, W. Cameron. 1945. *The Philippine Islands.* Cambridge: Harvard University Press.

Friend, Theodore. 1965. *Between two empires: The ordeal of the Philippines, 1929–1946.* New Haven: Yale University Press.

García, Mauro, ed. 1969. *Aguinaldo in retrospect.* Manila: Philippine Historical Commission.

Gates, John M. 1973. *Schoolbooks and krags: The United States Army in the Philippines, 1898–1902.* Westport, Conn.: Greenwood Press.

Gemelli Carreri, Giovanni Franceso. 1963. *A voyage to the Philippines.* Manila: Filipiniana Book Guild.

Golay, Frank H., ed. 1966. *Philippine-American relations.* Manila: Solidaridad.

Grunder, Garel A., and William E. Livezey. 1951. *The Philippines and the United States.* Norman, Okla.: University of Oklahoma Press.

Guerrero, Leon Ma. 1969. *The first Filipino: A biography of José Rizal.* Manila: National Historical Commission.

Hayden, Joseph R. 1942. *The Philippines: A study in national development.* New York: Macmillan.

Ileto, Reynaldo C. 1970. *Magindanao, 1860–1888: The career of Datu Uto of Buayan.* Master's thesis. Cornell University, New York.

Jagor, Fedor. 1965. *Travels in the Philippines.* Manila: Filipiniana Book Guild.

Kalaw, Máximo M. 1926. *The development of Philippine politics, 1872–1920.* Manila: Oriental Commercial.

Karnow, Stanley. 1989. *In our image: America's empire in the Philippines.* New York: Random House.

Kerkvliet, Benedict. 1977. *The Huk rebellion: A study of peasant revolt in the Philippines.* Berkeley: University of California Press.

La Gironìere, Paul P. de. 1962. *Twenty years in the Philippines.* Manila: Filipiniana Book Guild.

Lachica, Eduardo. 1971. *Huk: Philippine agrarian society in revolt.* Manila: Solidaridad.

Le Gentil, Guillaume. 1964. *A voyage to the Indian seas.* Trans. F. C. Fischer. Manila: Filipiniana Book Guild.

Le Roy, James A. 1914. *The Americans in the Philippines.* 2 vols. Boston: Houghton Mifflin.

Liang, Dapen. 1970. *Philippine political parties and politics.* San Francisco.

Lichauco, Marcial P. 1952. *Roxas: The story of a great Filipino and of the political era in which he lived.* Manila.

Linn, Brian M. 1989. *The U.S. Army and counterinsurgency in the Philippines War, 1899–1902.* Chapel Hill: University of North Carolina Press.

Llorente, Ana María M. 1983. *A blending of cultures: The Batanes, 1686–1898.* Manila: Historical Conservation Society.

Majul, César Adib. 1973 *Muslims in the Philippines.* Quezon City: University of the Philippines Press.

Malay, Armando J. 1967. *Occupied Philippines: The role of Jorge B. Vargas during the Japanese occupation.* Manila: Filipiniana Book Guild.

Mallari, Francisco A. 1990. *Ibalon under storm and siege: Essays on Bicol history, 1565–1860.* Cagayan de Oro City: Xavier University.

Marche, Alfred. 1970. *Luzon and Palawan.* Trans. C. Ojeda & J. Castro. Manila: Filipiniana Book Guild.

May, Glenn Anthony. 1979. Filipino resistance to American occupation: Batangas, 1899–1902. *PHR* 48:532–56.

_____. 1981. The zones of Batangas. *PS* 29:89–103.

_____. 1984. *Social engineering in the Philippines: The aims, execution, and impact of American colonial policy, 1900–1913.* Quezon City: New Day.

McCoy, Alfred W., and Ed C. de Jesús, eds. 1982. *Philippine social history: Global trade and local transformations.* Quezon City: Ateneo de Manila University Press.

Medina, Juan de. 1903–09. History of the Augustinian order in the Philippines. In *BR* 23:119–297, 24:29–179.

Morga, Antonio de. 1903–09. Sucesos de las Islas Filipinas. In *BR* 15–16.

Morison, Samuel E. 1942. *Admiral of the ocean sea: A life of Christopher Columbus.* 2 vols. Boston: Little Brown.

Murillo Velarde, Pedro. 1903–09. Jesuit missions in the seventeenth century. In *BR* 45:27–119.

Noone, Martín J. 1981. *The islands saw it: The discovery and conquest of the Philippines, 1521–1581.* Dublin: Helicon Press.

Owen, Norman G. 1984. *Prosperity without progress: Manila hemp and material life in the colonial Philippines.* Quezon City: Ateneo de Manila University Press.

Owen, Norman, G., et al. 1972. *Compadre colonialism: Philippine-American relations, 1898–1946.* Manila: Solidaridad.

Phelan, John L. 1967. *The Hispanization of the Philippines: Spanish aims and Filipino responses, 1565–1700.* Madison: University of Wisconsin.

Pier, Arthur S. 1950. *American apostles to the Philippines.* Boston: Beacon Press.

Pigafetta, Antonio. 1903–09. Magellan's voyage around the world. In *BR* 33:25–366, 34:39–180.

Pomeroy, William J. 1963. *The forest.* New York: International.

_____. 1970. *American neo-colonialism: Its emergence in the Philippines and Asia.* New York: International.

Quiason, Serafín D. 1966. *English "country trade" with the Philippines, 1644–1765.* Quezon City: University of the Philippines Press.

_____. 1985. The tiangui: A preliminary view of an indigenous rural marketing system in the Spanish Philippines. *PS* 33:22–38.

Repetti, William C. 1940. *The beginning of Jesuit education in the Philippines: The College of Manila.* Manila: Manila.

_____. 1947. *The College of San José of Manila.* Manila: Manila Observatory.

Reuter, Frank T. 1967. *Catholic influence on American colonial policies, 1898–1904.* Austin: University of Texas Press.

Reynolds, Quentin J., and Geoffrey Bocca. 1965. *Macapagal, the incorruptible.* New York: McKay.

Robinson, John L. 1966. The history of acquisition: Foundations for misunderstanding. *PS* 14:131–40.

Robles, Eliodoro G. 1969. *The Philippines in the nineteenth century.* Quezon City: Malaya Books.

Salamanca, Bonifacio S. 1984. *The Filipino reaction to American rule, 1901–1913.* Quezon City: New Day.

Saulo, Alfredo B. 1990. *Communism in the Philippines: An introduction.* Quezon City: Ateneo de Manila University Press.

Schumacher, John N. 1972. *Father José Burgos, priest and nationalist.* Quezon City: Published for the Knights of Columbus by the Ateneo de Manila University Press.

_____. 1973. *The Propaganda Movement, 1880–1895*. Manila: Solidaridad.

_____. 1991. *The making of a nation*. Quezon City: Ateneo de Manila University Press.

Schurz, William L. 1939. *The Manila galleon*. New York: E. P. Dutton.

Scott, William H. 1979. Class structure in the unhispanized Philippines. *PS* 27:137–59.

_____. 1980. Filipino class structure in the sixteenth century. *PS* 28:142–75.

_____. 1984. *Prehispanic source materials for the study of Philippine history*. Revised ed. Quezon City: New Day.

_____. 1986. *Ilocano responses to American aggression, 1900–1901*. Quezon City: New Day.

Shalom, Stephen R. 1980. Philippine acceptance of the Bell Trade Act of 1946. *PHR* 49:499–517.

Smith, Robert Aura. 1958. *Philippine freedom, 1946–1958*. New York: Columbia University Press.

Stanley, Peter W. 1974. *A nation in the making*. Cambridge: Harvard University Press.

Taruc, Luis. 1967. *He who rides the tiger*. London: Chapman.

Taylor, George E. 1964. *The Philippines and the United States: Problems of partnership*. New York: Published for the Council on Foreign Relations by Praeger.

Taylor, John R. M. 1971. *The Philippine insurrection against the United States: A compilation of documents with notes and introduction*. 5 vols. Pasay City: Eugenio Lopez Foundation.

Tormo Sanz, Leandro. 1973. *1872*. Trans. Antonio M. Molina. Manila: Historical Conservation Society.

U.S. Philippine Commission. 1900–1901. *Reports of the Philippine Commission*. 8 vols. Washington, D.C.: Government Printing Office.

Villarroel, Fidel. 1971. *Father José Burgos, university student*. Manila: University of Santo Tomás.

_____. 1984. *José Rizal and the University of Santo Tomás*. Manila: University of Santo Tomás.

Welch, Richard E., Jr. 1979. *Response to imperialism*. Chapel Hill: University of North Carolina Press.

Wernstedt, Frederick L., and J. E. Spencer. 1978. *The Philippine island world: A physical, cultural, and regional geography*. Berkeley: University of California Press.

Wickberg, Edgar. 1965. *The Chinese in Philippine life, 1850–1898*. New Haven: Yale University Press.